DANNY PROULX

BUILDING WOODSHOP WORKSTATIONS

POPULAR WOODWORKING BOOKS

CINCINNATI, OHIO
www.popularwoodworking.com

Read This Important Safety Notice

To prevent accidents, keep safety in mind while you work. Use the safety guards installed on power equipment; they are for your protection. When working on power equipment, keep fingers away from saw blades, wear safety goggles to prevent injuries from flying wood chips and sawdust, wear headphones to protect your hearing, and consider installing a dust vacuum to reduce the amount of airborne sawdust in your woodshop. Don't wear loose clothing, such as neckties or shirts with loose sleeves, or jewelry, such as rings, necklaces or bracelets, when working on power equipment. Tie back long hair to prevent it from getting caught in your equipment. People who are sensitive to certain chemicals should check the chemical content of any product before using it. The authors and editors who compiled this book have tried to make the contents as accurate and correct as possible. Plans, illustrations, photographs and text have been carefully checked. All instructions, plans and projects should be carefully read, studied and understood before beginning construction. In some photos, power tool guards have been removed to more clearly show the operation being demonstrated. Always use all safety guards and attachments that come with your power tools. Due to the variability of local conditions, construction materials, skill levels, etc., neither the author nor Popular Woodworking Books assumes any responsibility for any accidents, injuries, damages or other losses incurred resulting from the material presented in this book. Prices listed for supplies and equipment were current at the time of publication and are subject to change. Glass shelving should have all edges polished and must be tempered. Untempered glass shelves may shatter and can cause serious bodily injury. Tempered shelves are very strong and if they break will just crumble, minimizing personal injury.

Metric Conversion Chart

TO CONVERT	TO	MULTIPLY BY
Inches	Centimeters	2.54
Centimeters	Inches	0.4
Feet	Centimeters	30.5
Centimeters	Feet	0.03
Yards	Meters	0.9
Meters	Yards	1.1
Sq. Inches	Sq. Centimeters	6.45
Sq. Centimeters	Sq. Inches	0.16
Sq. Feet	Sq. Meters	0.09
Sq. Meters	Sq. Feet	10.8
Sq. Yards	Sq. Meters	0.8
Sq. Meters	Sq. Yards	1.2
Pounds	Kilograms	0.45
Kilograms	Pounds	2.2
Ounces	Grams	28.4
Grams	Ounces	0.035

Building Woodshop Workstations. Copyright © 2002 by Danny Proulx. Manufactured in China. All rights reserved. No part of this book may be reproduced in any form or by any electronic or mechanical means including information storage and retrieval systems without permission in writing from the publisher, except by a reviewer, who may quote brief passages in a review. Published by Popular Woodworking Books, an imprint of F&W Publications, Inc., 4700 East Galbraith Road, Cincinnati, Ohio, 45236. 800-289-0963. First edition.

Visit our Web site at www.popularwoodworking.com for information on more resources for woodworkers.

Other fine Popular Woodworking Books are available from your local bookstore or direct from the publisher.

07   06   05   04   03   5   4   3   2   1

Library of Congress Cataloging-in-Publication Data

Proulx, Danny, 1947-
  Building Woodshop Workstations / by Danny Proulx.-- 1st ed.
     p. cm.
  ISBN 1-55870-637-2
  1. Cabinetwork. 2. Woodworking tools. 3. Workshops--Design and construction. I. Title.
  TT197 .P78 2003
  684'.083--dc21
                              2002011005

ACQUISITIONS EDITOR: Jim Stack
EDITOR: Jennifer Ziegler
DESIGNER: Brian Roeth
PRODUCTION COORDINATOR: Mark Griffin
PAGE LAYOUT ARTIST: Christine Long
Step-by-step photography by Danny Proulx
Cover and chapter lead photography by Michael Bowie, Lux Photography, 2450 Lancaster Rd., Suite 25, Ottawa, Ontario, K1B 4S5, 613-247-7199
Technical illustrations by Len Churchill, Lenmark Communications, Ltd., 590 Alden Rd., Suite 206, Markham, Ontario, L3R 8N2, 905-475-5222
Workshop site at Rideau Cabinets, P.O. Box 331, Russell, Ontario, K4R 1E1, 613-445-3722

About the Author

Danny Proulx has been involved in the woodworking field for more than 30 years. He has operated a custom kitchen cabinet shop since 1989. Danny also teaches full-time and continuing-education students at Algonquin College in Ottawa, Ontario.

He is a contributing editor to *Cabinet-Maker* magazine and has published articles in other magazines such as *Canadian Home Workshop*, *Canadian Woodworking*, *Popular Woodworking*, *Woodshop News* and *Canadian Homes and Cottages*.

His earlier books include *Build Your Own Kitchen Cabinets*, *The Kitchen Cabinetmaker's Building and Business Manual*, *How to Build Classic Garden Furniture*, *Smart Shelving & Storage Solutions*, *Fast and Easy Techniques for Building Modern Cabinetry*, *Building More Classic Garden Furniture*, *Building Cabinet Doors & Drawers*, *Build Your Own Home Office Furniture* and *Display Cases You Can Build*. You can reach Danny either through his Web site, www.cabinetmaking.com, or via e-mail at danny@cabinetmaking.com.

Acknowledgements

Many suppliers have contributed products, materials and technical support during the project-building phase of this book, including Delta, Porter-Cable, Exaktor Tools and so many others.

I appreciate how helpful they've been and recommend these companies without hesitation. A complete list of suppliers is listed at the end of this book.

Dedication

This book is another team effort. I couldn't meet deadlines, build and write without the dedicated help of my wife, Gale, and my friend Jack Chaters, who is always ready when needed. The master of photographic art, Michael Bowie of Lux Photography in Ottawa, is the wizard behind the images. He is always ready to lift, push, pull, carry anything or meet me anywhere to get the best photograph possible. I couldn't meet deadlines without Michael's help.

Len Churchill, of Lenmark Communications in Markham, has again provided the exploded views. Len is a genius with illustrations, and I'm lucky to have the talents of a first-class illustrator who is also very knowledgeable in the woodworking field. I send Len a few pictures, some measurements and a few quick notes, and he turns all that mess into something beautiful.

The staff at Popular Woodworking Books is my support team, and I'm very lucky to have such a talented and dedicated group of professionals. They include Jim Stack, Jenny Ziegler, Brian Roeth and Mark Griffin. They are all ready to help at a moment's notice. Thank you!

Thanks are also due to all the readers of my books who have sent pictures of completed projects, comments, suggestions and tips of their own for me to use. I truly appreciate your time and efforts.

table of contents

introduction . . . 6

suppliers . . . 127

index . . . 128

ROUTER TABLE CABINET

SHOP-MADE 12" DISC SANDER

MOBILE TABLE SAW CENTER

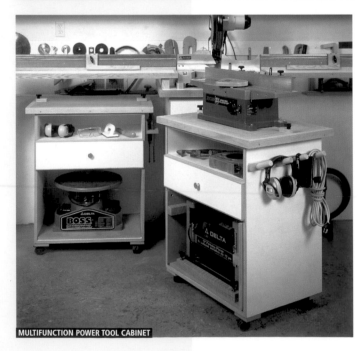

MULTIFUNCTION POWER TOOL CABINET

PROJECTS

ONE

Base- and Wall-Mounted Workshop Cabinets . . . 8

TWO

The Practical Workbench . . . 18

THREE

Power Miter Saw Station . . . 28

FOUR

Multifunction Power Tool Cabinet . . . 40

FIVE

Power Tool Storage Station . . . 48

SIX

Mobile Table Saw Center . . . 54

SEVEN

Router Table Cabinet . . . 68

MOBILE WORKBENCH AND TOOL CABINET

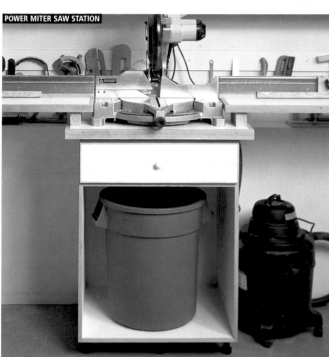

POWER MITER SAW STATION

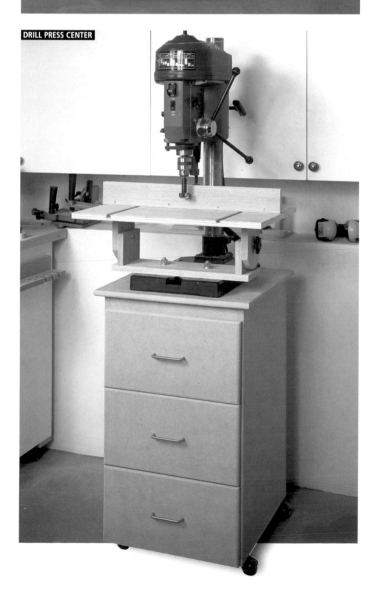

DRILL PRESS CENTER

EIGHT

Drill Press Center . . . 80

NINE

Tool Sharpening and Maintenance Station . . . 90

TEN

Mobile Workbench and Tool Cabinet . . . 100

ELEVEN

Saw Outfeed Table and Storage Cabinet . . . 110

TWELVE

Shop-Made 12" Disc Sander . . . 118

introduction

Maximizing space, creating multifunctional tool stations and increasing shop efficiency are the goals of this book. These three criteria will impact the design of each project.

Woodworkers are bombarded with ads from tool manufacturers. Each year we see dozens of new power tools, many of which are benchtop units. Oscillating sanders, planers, joiners, scroll saws, power miter saws and so on, are must-haves for a woodworker's shop. However, most home workshops suffer from one common problem — a lack of space. You'll often find the garage or basement filled with tools, leaving very little free space to work.

Power tool stations can be multifunctional because you don't need a great number of tools for most projects. Building multiuse tool stations has become popular because they serve a number of operations in the woodshop. This book will show different tool stations that can serve a number of power tools.

The other serious issue confronting the home woodworker is the requirement to share space. A woodworking shop in a garage is typical of that situation. A number of tools, like the router table, for example, can be static stations because they can be used against a wall. Tools that must be used with clearance on all sides, however, such as a table saw, have to be movable. To meet the needs of a shared space, a number of these projects will be movable.

The power miter saw station is a major player in the space efficiency design issue throughout this book. It is a center tower with "wings" to support long boards at the saw station. The wings are constructed at a height that will allow the multifunction power tool cabinets to be rolled underneath for storage. A number of the other portable tool stations will be designed to fit under the miter saw station.

The first chapter deals with base and wall cabinets, because storage is a key element when creating an efficient shop. The next chapter details a workbench that not only is functional, but also recovers valuable floor space under the bench. Space recovery and maximizing every square inch of a workshop is the goal, and projects like the Power Tool Storage Station and the Saw Outfeed Table and Storage Cabinet meet that objective. The Mobile Table Saw Center and the Router Table Cabinet address the work efficiency needs of two important shop power tools.

I hope you build a number of these projects and they help increase the joy you get by working in your woodshop. As someone often repeated to me when I was young, "The trick is to work smarter, not harder."

Base- and Wall-Mounted Workshop Cabinets

Good-quality storage cabinets with doors are just as important as any power tool workstation in your shop. They store all types of tools and hardware, organize your materials and prolong the life of your tools. The base cabinets also serve as a support medium for countertops. That's a pretty good deal for a few dollars' worth of sheet material and a handful of screws.

The cabinets detailed in this chapter are frameless-style cabinetry. Unlike the traditional-styled cabinet, they don't have a wooden face frame installed.

The base cabinets are different from wall cabinets because they don't have a top board, but they do require a top rail to provide countertop overhang clearance. Both are built following the same simple principles.

The selection of sheet materials used to build your shop cabinets is a personal choice. Almost any material can be used as long as it's ⅝" or thicker, and of reasonable quality. I've chosen

white melamine-coated particleboard (PB) for a number of reasons.

First, the PB is coated, making it easy to clean. Secondly, the doors can be made from the same material without the need to apply a finish and the edges can be finished with iron-on tape. Finally, the white cabinets reflect almost all the light that strikes them, helping to illuminate the shop.

The cabinets will be sturdy and long-lasting if you properly join the particleboard with the correct fasteners, and the edges will be chip free if you use the correct saw blade.

These cabinets can be fitted with drawers, pullouts in the base units and adjustable shelves. They are constructed using bottom-mounted drawer glides, adjustable legs and hidden hinges. The end result will be a high-quality cabinet at a reasonable cost.

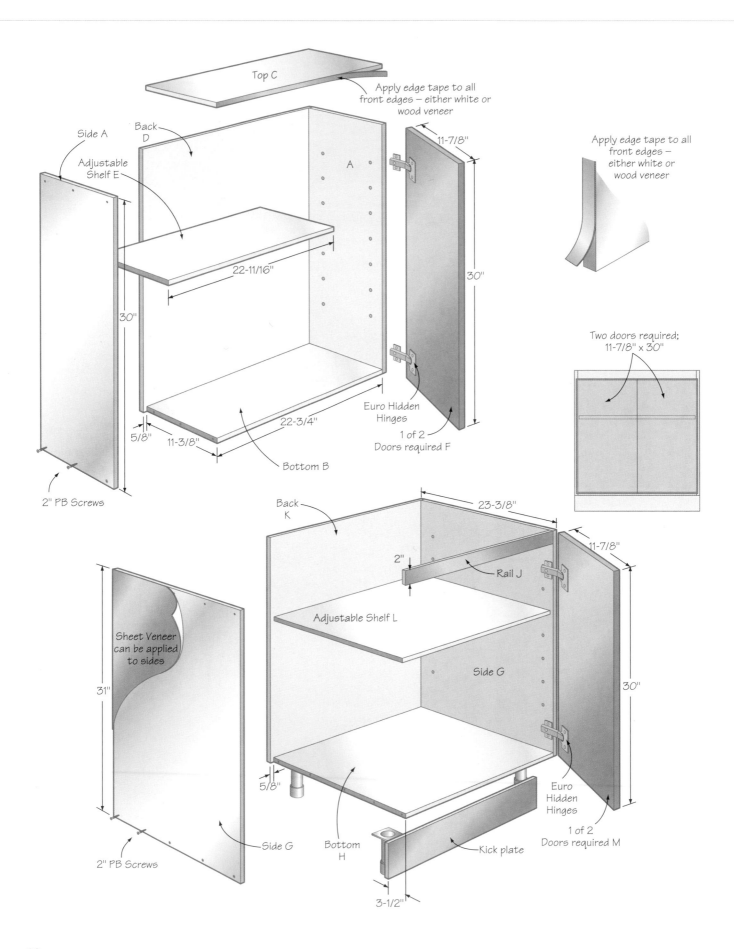

Top C

Apply edge tape to all
front edges – either white or
wood veneer

Back
D

Side A

Adjustable
Shelf E

A

11-7/8"

Apply edge tape to all
front edges –
either white or
wood veneer

30"

22-11/16"

30"

30"

Euro Hidden
Hinges

1 of 2
Doors required F

Two doors required;
11-7/8" x 30"

2" PB Screws

5/8"

11-3/8"

22-3/4"

Bottom B

Back
K

23-3/8"

11-7/8"

2"

Rail J

Adjustable Shelf L

Side G

30"

Sheet Veneer
can be applied
to sides

31"

5/8"

Euro
Hidden
Hinges

1 of 2
Doors required M

2" PB Screws

Side G

Bottom
H

Kick plate

3-1/2"

REFERENCE	QUANTITY	PART	STOCK	THICKNESS	WIDTH	LENGTH	COMMENTS
24"-WIDE WALL CABINET							
A	2	sides	melamine PB	$5/8$	$11^3/8$	30	
B	1	bottom	melamine PB	$5/8$	$11^3/8$	$22^3/4$	
C	1	top	melamine PB	$5/8$	$11^3/8$	$22^3/4$	
D	1	back	melamine PB	$5/8$	24	30	
E	2	shelves	melamine PB	$5/8$	$11^3/8$	$22^{11}/16$	
F	2	doors	melamine PB	$5/8$	$11^7/8$	30	
24"-WIDE BASE CABINET							
G	2	sides	melamine PB	$5/8$	$23^3/8$	31	
H	1	bottom	melamine PB	$5/8$	$23^3/8$	$22^3/4$	
J	1	top rail	melamine PB	$5/8$	2	$22^3/4$	
K	1	back	melamine PB	$5/8$	24	31	
L	1	shelf	melamine PB	$5/8$	$23^3/8$	$22^{11}/16$	
M	2	doors	melamine PB	$5/8$	$11^7/8$	30	

HARDWARE

Edge tape
Shelf pins
2" PB screws
Hidden hinges
$5/8$" PB screws
3" Screws
1" Screws
Right-angle brackets
Adjustable cabinet legs
Plinth clip
Drawer glides
Drawer handles
Door handles

REFERENCE	QUANTITY	PART	STOCK	THICKNESS	WIDTH	LENGTH	COMMENTS
610MM-WIDE WALL CABINET							
A	2	sides	melamine PB	16	289	762	
B	1	bottom	melamine PB	16	289	578	
C	1	top	melamine PB	16	289	578	
D	1	back	melamine PB	16	610	762	
E	2	shelves	melamine PB	16	289	577	
F	2	doors	melamine PB	16	301	762	
610MM-WIDE BASE CABINET							
G	2	sides	melamine PB	16	594	787	
H	1	bottom	melamine PB	16	594	578	
J	1	top rail	melamine PB	16	51	578	
K	1	back	melamine PB	16	610	787	
L	1	shelf	melamine PB	16	594	577	
M	2	doors	melamine PB	16	301	762	

HARDWARE

Edge tape
Shelf pins
51mm PB screws
Hidden hinges
16mm PB screws
76mm Screws
25mm Screws
Right-angle brackets
Adjustable cabinet legs
Plinth clip
Drawer glides
Drawer handles
Door handles

Shop Tip

Both wall and base cabinet materials lists are based on using $5/8$"-thick melamine particleboard.

Wall cabinets are usually 12"-deep by 30"-high. Base cabinets are 24"-deep by $35^1/4$"-high. Adding a $3/4$"-thick top to the base cabinet means the top surface will be 36" from the floor. If you want a different height, alter the height of the back and side boards.

BUILDING A 24" WALL CABINET

Calculating Cabinet Door Sizes

The size of cabinet doors that will be mounted on hidden hinges (100°-opening, full-overlay hinges) can be easily calculated. First, measure the inside dimension of the cabinet to be fitted with doors.

A 24"-wide cabinet, built using the materials list shown for this project, has an inside dimension of $22^3/4$" (24"-wide cabinet minus two $5/8$" side thicknesses). Add 1" to this measurement and that's the required door width. In this example, the door width would be $23^3/4$", which is a little too wide. Door widths should be less than 18" wide if possible.

I can install two doors that are $11^7/8$" wide in place of the $23^3/4$" door. The width for each of the two doors is found by adding 1" to the inside cabinet dimension, then dividing by 2.

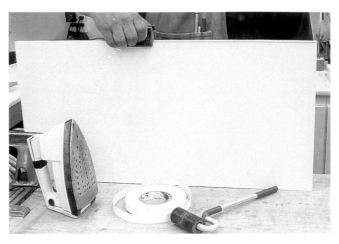

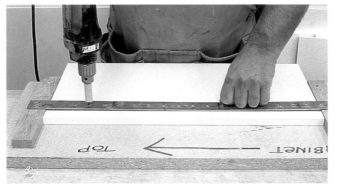

STEP 2 ■ Holes for the adjustable shelves are drilled in the cabinet sides before assembly. I use a simple jig made with a flat steel bar and wooden blocks mounted to a small sheet of plywood. The drill bit's travel is limited by a piece of dowel on the drill bit. My shelf pins are 5mm ($3/16$") in diameter. Holes in the steel bar on my jig are 5mm in diameter and spaced $1^1/4$" apart. Drill as many holes as you require. The spacing isn't critical but be sure you know the diameter of your shelf-pin holes before drilling.

STEP 1 ■ The exposed edges of all cabinet parts must be covered. I use a heat-activated edge tape and apply it with an old household iron. Run a small roller along the tape surface before the glue cools and dries to properly seat the tape. Excess edge tape can be trimmed with a sharp chisel or double-edged trimmer that is available at woodworking stores.

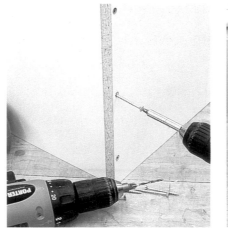

STEP 3 ■ Attach the two side boards A to the bottom B and top C using 2" PB screws. Drill a pilot hole for each screw and align the bottom and top boards with the top and bottom edges of the sides.

STEP 4 ■ The full-thickness back D should be as wide and as high as the cabinet. It is attached using 2" PB screws in drilled holes spaced about 6" apart.

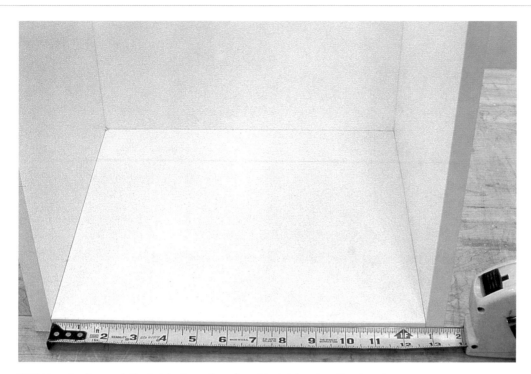

Cabinet Sizes

The dimensions for a cabinet of any width from 10" to 36" can easily be calculated. Begin your calculations by deciding the final cabinet width. If a 33"-wide wall cabinet is needed, I subtract the two $\frac{5}{8}$" side thicknesses from the total width needed to find my bottom and top board dimensions. Thus, they would have to be $31\frac{3}{4}$" wide by the standard $11\frac{3}{8}$" deep. The backboard size equals the total width and height of the cabinet, or 33" wide by 30" high.

Determine the door sizes as previously detailed, install hinges and the cabinet is complete. Follow the construction steps for all cabinets, no matter how wide.

STEP 5 ▪ As discussed, the inside dimension of a cabinet determines the door size when using full-overlay hidden hinges. Adding 1" to the interior width and dividing by 2 means I will need two $11\frac{7}{8}$"-wide doors F. Upper frameless cabinet doors normally cover the edges of the top and bottom board, and are the same height as the cabinet.

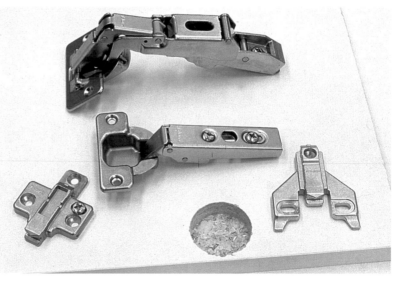

STEP 6 ▪ Apply heat-activated edge tape to all four edges of each door. Using a flat-bottomed hinge-boring bit in a drill press, drill two 35mm-diameter holes into each door to accept the hidden-hinge assemblies. The holes are normally located 4" from each end and $\frac{1}{8}$" from the door's edge.

STEP 7 ▪ The standard hidden hinge is a full-overlay 100°–120°-opening hinge. The term full-overlay refers to the door position when attached with this hinge. It will overlay or cover the side end edge by almost $\frac{5}{8}$". The mounting plate attaches to the cabinet side. The standard hinge is shown in the middle, and the mounting plate that is commonly used is shown on the left.

The top hinge is a 170°-opening model, and the mounting plate on the right is used to attach the hinge to a face frame.

Basic Construction Principles of Frameless Cabinetry

Frameless cabinetry is strong and sturdy when properly constructed, however, you should use quality materials such as cabinet-grade melamine particleboard. To be designated cabinet-grade, the board must have a high-quality core material and a melamine layer. Inexpensive board isn't a low-pressure laminate type and often has a melamine layer that's painted or glued.

The cabinet parts are joined with special fasteners, like the ones used in this project, such as the particleboard screw. Drill pilot holes for all screws to achieve the maximum hold.

Melamine particleboard is available in different thicknesses. The $5/8$" and $3/4$" sizes are the most common, so use whichever size is readily available in your area. I will be using $5/8$"-thick material, but if you decide to use $3/4$", or that's all there is available in your area, follow the same process as previously described to determine cut sizes. The steps are the same no matter which thickness is used. The cabinet width, minus the side thicknesses in total, equals the bottom and top board width, and so on.

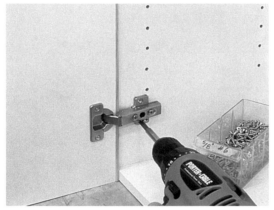

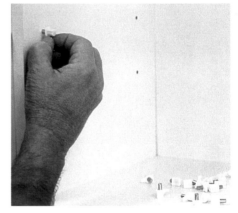

STEP 8 ■ Use $5/8$" particleboard screws to secure both hinges to the door. Align the hinge body with a square to ensure it's parallel to the door edge.

STEP 9 ■ Attach the hinge plate on the hinge body and align the door (in its normally open position) against the cabinet. Place a $1/8$"-thick spacer between the door edge and the cabinet edge. Next, drive $5/8$" PB screws through the holes in the hinge plate to secure the door.

This is a simple and accurate alignment procedure for mounting doors with hidden hinges without measuring or using jigs. The procedure will work only with 100° to 120° full-overlay hidden hinges. If you want to install the wider 170°-opening hinges, follow the procedures for using a 100° to 120° hinge. Once the hinge plate is secured, remove the standard hinge and install the wide-opening model on the door. The mounting plate is correctly located for all hinges but must be installed using the standard-opening model.

STEP 10 ■ Mount the cabinets to the wall using 3"-long screws driven into wall studs. If you have a series of cabinets, secure the front edges to each other with 1" screws. Complete the installation by installing the shelves E on shelf pins in the drilled holes.

BUILDING A 24" BASE CABINET

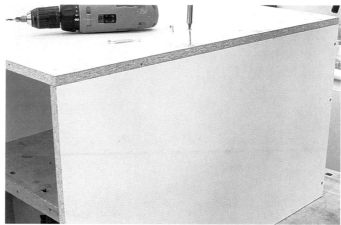

STEP 11 ■ Apply tape to all exposed panel edges as detailed in previous steps. If you plan on having adjustable shelves in your base cabinet, drill the holes at this point. Attach the cabinet sides G to the bottom board H using 2" PB screws.

STEP 12 ■ A base cabinet does not require a top board because the cabinet will be covered with a counter or other work surface. Attach the backboard K making sure the bottom and sides are aligned flush to the outside edges. Drill pilot holes and attach the backboard with 2" PB screws 6" to 8" apart.

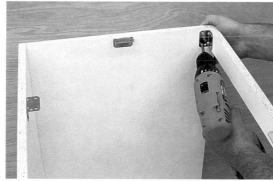

STEP 13 ■ A 2"-high upper rail J must be installed on a frameless base cabinet. This will provide overhang clearance for the countertop and doors. The 30"-high doors are 1" below the top edge of this rail. Use one 2" PB screw per end. Drive the screw into a pilot hole that's located as close to the center of the rail as possible.

STEP 14 ■ Install right-angle brackets to strengthen the upper rail. One bracket per end using $5/8$" screws will support the rail. The other brackets installed on the base will be used to secure the countertop. The number of brackets required will vary with cabinet size; however, one every 12" apart will be adequate to secure the counter.

STEP 15 ■ I use adjustable cabinet legs on most of my base cabinets. I don't have to build a base frame, and the legs are adjustable for easier cabinet installation. The legs are plastic, so water and other liquids that sometimes spill in the shop do not affect them. Cabinet legs are secured with $5/8$" screws and are set 3" back from the front edge of the cabinet.

STEP 16 ■ Kick plates aren't necessary with shop cabinets, but if you want to use them, they can be attached with a plinth clip. This piece of hardware is designed to secure kick plates to cabinet legs with spring clips.

Finally, complete the base by installing cabinet doors M. They are 30" high and are located 1" below the top edge of the cabinet rail. The space above both doors is used to provide clearance for a countertop. Follow the same procedures as detailed for building the wall cabinet.

BUILDING DRAWERS

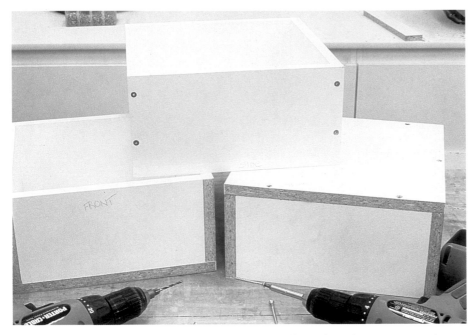

STEP 17 ■ Tip an upper cabinet on its back and you have a drawer box. The same construction procedures are used for both units. Drawer boxes don't need adjustable shelf holes or doors, but they are identical to upper cabinets in every other way.

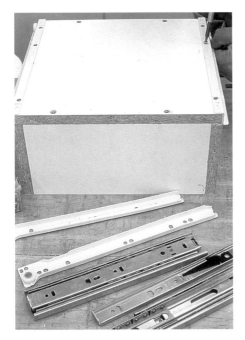

STEP 18 ■ Drawer boxes can be mounted with many glide systems. I use $\frac{3}{4}$-extension glides (a 22" drawer box pulls out about 15") and full-extension glides (the 22" drawer box comes all the way out). The full-extension (FX) glides mount on the drawer box side, and the $\frac{3}{4}$-type glides mount on the drawer bottom and side. Both styles require a $\frac{1}{2}$" clearance on each side of the box between the cabinet sides. The clearance dimensions required with most glide systems are critical, so accurate cutting of parts is important. The FX glides (chrome model in picture) are used when full access to the drawer box is needed, but they are about three times more expensive than the standard $\frac{3}{4}$-extension models.

STEP 19 ■ Follow the manufacturer's instructions when installing drawer glides. Most of the drawer hardware on the market can be installed by drawing a guideline inside the cabinet using a carpenter's square. The square's tongue is held tight to the cabinet's face so the guideline will be at a perfect right angle to the side board's front edge.

Frameless cabinets do not have rails, so it can be tricky calculating drawer box sizes with a multiple bank of drawers. A good rule is to leave 1" of space below and above each drawer box. That means there will be a 2" space between drawer boxes because each one requires that 1" clearance above and below.

Each drawer box height can be found by dividing the number of boxes needed into the final space available. I will need three boxes approximately $7\frac{1}{2}$" high ($22\frac{3}{8}$" divided by 3). Or, I can have any combination of three box heights that equal $22\frac{3}{8}$" high. You may want two large bottom drawers at 9" each and a small top-drawer box that's $4\frac{3}{8}$" high. Any combination of sizes is fine as long as the 1" clearance above and below the drawer box is respected.

These cabinets are a handy addition to any workshop. The wall cabinets are easily secured using 3" screws into the studs. Screws can be driven anywhere through the cabinet backboard because it's full thickness. It's an incredibly strong cabinet design that can stand alone without any added support.

The base cabinets stand on plastic legs and will accept a dozen different countertop or work-surface styles. You can use plywood with a coat of paint or a fancier laminate-covered top. Countertops or work surfaces for the base cabinets can be built in many ways. The design depends on your needs. I'll build different work surfaces throughout the book and you can select the style that's best for you.

You aren't limited to melamine particleboard when building these cabinets. Sheet goods such as medium-density fiberboard (MDF), plywood or plain particleboard are all fine. Low-cost sheet material can be protected with a good coat of paint.

STEP 20 ▪ The drawer face is similar to a door because all four edges must be covered with tape. The width of each drawer face is 1" greater than the inside dimension of the cabinet; the same calculation is used to find door widths. The height of drawer faces is determined by the position of the free space above each drawer box.

Here is an easy way to accurately locate drawer faces on the drawer box. First, determine which handles or pulls will be used and drill the mounting holes in the drawer face only. Install the drawer boxes. Position the drawer face on the cabinet and drive a screw through the handle holes into the drawer box. The face is located and secured properly, so you can pull out the drawer and install screws from the interior of the drawer box into the back of the drawer face. Now remove the screws from the front of the drawer face and finish drilling the handle holes. Finally, install the handles.

The Practical Workbench

I'm sure there are one hundred ways to build a workbench, and all of them are correct if they meet your needs. Here's a workbench that fills all my requirements and one that will hopefully be useful in your workshop.

A bench doesn't have to be pretty. A good hardwood that's straight and flat, with a few blemishes, is just fine. After all, we're going to be pounding, clamping, dragging and abusing the top in the years to come. The bench should be strong and heavy enough to withstand a bit of pushing and pulling when we are working wood.

I used ash for my bench and tried to keep the best faces for my top surface. Even though I selected the wood carefully, I did have a few little checks and knots to fill. This wood wasn't a select grade, so I didn't expect perfection. Carefully sort through the lesser grades of lumber and pick the best pieces for your bench. It may not win a beauty contest, but the price will be a lot less than select-grade lumber.

A bench needs one or two good vises and, since a bench has a great deal of space below, a storage cabinet for frequently used tools. This bench has five drawers for tools and a shelf for tucking those tools aside when you are working on a project, keeping them within easy reach.

I installed two Veritas vises on my bench. The twin-screw model is a well-machined and very useful tool. The single-screw model mounted on the right side of the bench is perfect for my work. Both vises are available at Lee Valley Tools. The bench can be mounted on wheels, the vise styles and positions can be changed and the size can be altered for your shop. It's well worth your time and money to build a good workbench because it will be an important part of your shop for many years.

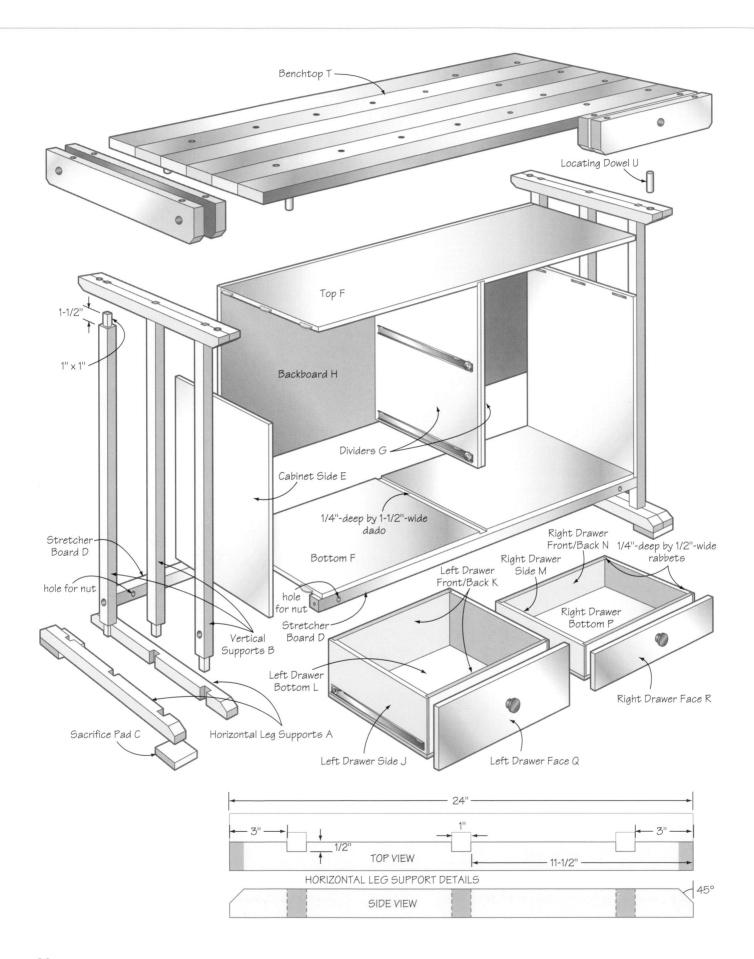

Benchtop T

Locating Dowel U

1-1/2"

1" x 1"

Top F

Backboard H

Dividers G

Cabinet Side E

1/4"-deep by 1-1/2"-wide dado

Bottom F

Right Drawer Front/Back N

Right Drawer Side M

1/4"-deep by 1/2"-wide rabbets

Left Drawer Front/Back K

Right Drawer Bottom P

Stretcher Board D

hole for nut

hole for nut

Stretcher Board D

Vertical Supports B

Left Drawer Bottom L

Right Drawer Face R

Sacrifice Pad C

Horizontal Leg Supports A

Left Drawer Side J

Left Drawer Face Q

24"

3"

1/2"

1"

3"

TOP VIEW

11-1/2"

HORIZONTAL LEG SUPPORT DETAILS

SIDE VIEW

45°

materials list ▪ **INCHES**

REFERENCE	QUANTITY	PART	STOCK	THICKNESS	WIDTH	LENGTH
A	8	horizontal supports	solid hardwood	$1\frac{1}{2}$	$1\frac{1}{2}$	24
B	6	vertical supports	solid hardwood	$1\frac{1}{2}$	$1\frac{1}{2}$	$33\frac{1}{2}$
C	4	sacrifice pads	solid hardwood	1	3	3
D	2	stretcher boards	solid hardwood	$1\frac{1}{2}$	$2\frac{1}{2}$	44
E	2	cabinet sides	veneer plywood	$\frac{3}{4}$	$16\frac{3}{4}$	20
F	2	bottom & top boards	veneer plywood	$\frac{3}{4}$	$16\frac{3}{4}$	$42\frac{1}{2}$
G	2	dividers	veneer plywood	$\frac{3}{4}$	$16\frac{3}{4}$	19
H	1	backboard	veneer plywood	$\frac{3}{4}$	20	44

TWO LEFT-SIDE DRAWER BOXES

J	4	sides	birch plywood	$\frac{1}{2}$	$6\frac{3}{4}$	16
K	4	fronts & backs	birch plywood	$\frac{1}{2}$	$6\frac{3}{4}$	19
L	2	bottoms	birch plywood	$\frac{1}{2}$	16	$19\frac{1}{2}$

THREE RIGHT-SIDE DRAWER BOXES

M	6	sides	birch plywood	$\frac{1}{2}$	$3\frac{5}{8}$	16
N	6	fronts & backs	birch plywood	$\frac{1}{2}$	$3\frac{5}{8}$	19
P	3	bottoms	birch plywood	$\frac{1}{2}$	16	$19\frac{1}{2}$

DRAWER FACES

Q	2	faces	veneer plywood	$\frac{3}{4}$	$9\frac{3}{4}$	$21\frac{1}{2}$
R	2	faces	veneer plywood	$\frac{3}{4}$	$6\frac{3}{4}$	$21\frac{1}{2}$
S	1	faces	veneer plywood	$\frac{3}{4}$	6	$21\frac{1}{2}$

BENCHTOP

T	1	benchtop	solid hardwood	$1\frac{1}{2}$	30	72
U	4	locating dowels	solid hardwood			
		(1" diameter by $2\frac{1}{2}$" long)				

HARDWARE

5 Sets of 18"-long, $\frac{3}{4}$-extension glides (use full-extension glides if desired)

Drawer handles or knobs

PB screws

Bolts, nuts and washers as detailed

Plate joinery biscuits (#20)

Glue

4" x $\frac{3}{8}$"-Diameter bolts with washers and nuts

Wood edge tape

$1\frac{1}{2}$" PB screws

1" Brad nails

$\frac{1}{2}$" Screws

1" Screws

OPTIONAL

1 Front vise (Veritas Tools by Lee Valley Tools #70G08.02)

1 Twin-screw vise (Veritas Tools by Lee Valley Tools #05G12.22)

4 Bench dogs (Veritas Tools by Lee Valley Tools #05G04.04)

---

materials list ▪ **MILLIMETERS**

REFERENCE	QUANTITY	PART	STOCK	THICKNESS	WIDTH	LENGTH
A	8	horizontal supports	solid hardwood	38	38	610
B	6	vertical supports	solid hardwood	38	38	851
C	4	sacrifice pads	solid hardwood	25	76	76
D	2	stretcher boards	solid hardwood	38	64	1118
E	2	cabinet sides	veneer plywood	19	425	508
F	2	bottom & top boards	veneer plywood	19	425	1080
G	2	dividers	veneer plywood	19	425	483
H	1	backboard	veneer plywood	1938	20	44

TWO LEFT-SIDE DRAWER BOXES

J	4	sides	birch plywood	13	171	406
K	4	fronts & backs	birch plywood	13	171	483
L	2	bottoms	birch plywood	13	406	496

THREE RIGHT-SIDE DRAWER BOXES

M	6	sides	birch plywood	13	92	406
N	6	fronts & backs	birch plywood	13	92	483
P	3	bottoms	birch plywood	13	406	496

DRAWER FACES

Q	2	faces	veneer plywood	19	248	546
R	2	faces	veneer plywood	19	171	546
S	1	faces	veneer plywood	19	152	546

BENCHTOP

T	1	benchtop	solid hardwood	38	762	1829
U	4	locating dowels	solid hardwood			
		(1" diameter by $2\frac{1}{2}$" long)				

HARDWARE

5 Sets of 457mm-long, $\frac{3}{4}$-extension glides (use full-extension glides if desired)

Drawer handles or knobs

PB screws

Bolts, nuts and washers as detailed

Plate joinery biscuits (#20)

Glue

102mm × 10mm-Diameter bolts with washers and nuts

Wood edge tape

38mm PB screws

25mm Brad nails

13mm Screws

25mm Screws

OPTIONAL

1 Front vise (Veritas Tools by Lee Valley Tools #70G08.02)

1 Twin-screw vise (Veritas Tools by Lee Valley Tools #05G12.22)

4 Bench dogs (Veritas Tools by Lee Valley Tools #05G04.04)

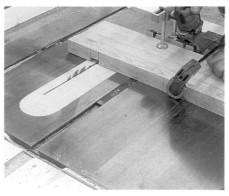

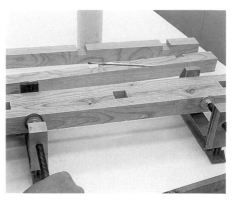

STEP 1 ■ Rip and crosscut the eight horizontal supports A at 1½"-square by 24"-long, and the six vertical supports B at 1½"-square by 33½"-long. A good crosscut blade on a table saw will be required to cut the 1½"-thick material. A sliding table on your table saw, a radial-arm saw or power miter box can be used to crosscut the parts.

STEP 2 ■ The eight horizontal supports A each require three dadoes that are 1"-wide by ½"-deep. Two of the dadoes are located 3" from each end, and the third is located directly in the center. Dadoes can be cut on a table saw. If possible, gang four pieces together at one time and mark the pairs; this will ensure that sets are matched for joining.

STEP 3 ■ Glue two horizontal supports A together, forming a board with three 1"-square through-mortises. The eight supports will make four horizontal support members. Use dowels, biscuits or simply edge-glue the pieces to each other.

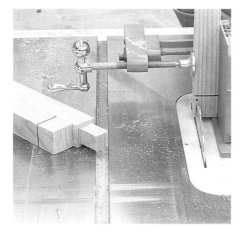

STEP 5 ■ Cut a 45° corner on the end of all four horizontal supports A. Use a ¼" roundover bit in your router to ease all the corners on the vertical supports B, and the top edges of the bottom two horizontal supports A. Don't round over the bottom of the lower horizontal supports that touch the floor or the two top horizontal supports.

STEP 4 ■ The six vertical supports B require a 1"-square by 1½"-long tenon centered on each end. These tenons can be cut on a table saw with a miter slide or, if you have one, a tenoning jig.

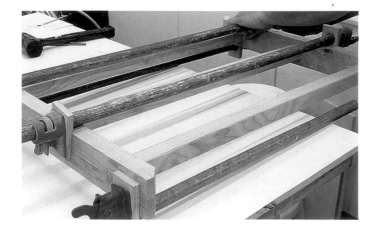

STEP 6 ■ Build both leg assemblies using glue and clamps. The tenons should fit snugly into the mortises. Set aside both leg units until the adhesive cures.

STEP 8 ■ Cut the two stretcher boards D to the size indicated in the materials list. Drill a 1"-diameter through-hole, centered 4" from each end on both stretchers. Then drill the ends of both boards using a ³⁄₈"-diameter bit. The holes are located on the center of each end and are drilled 4" deep to meet the 1"-diameter through-holes.

STEP 7 ■ To save wear and tear on the lower horizontal supports, install sacrifice pads. These are 3"-square by 1"-thick and are attached with screws only. When the pads wear because the bench is moved a great deal or become damaged by moisture or liquids on the floor, simply replace the pads.

STEP 9 ■ Drill a ¹⁄₂"-deep by 1"-diameter hole 4" above the bottom of each vertical support B. Center the hole on the four vertical uprights, making sure your measurements are from the bottom of the vertical supports and not the lower edge of the horizontal supports. Next, drill a ³⁄₈"-diameter through-hole in the center of each 1"-diameter hole for the assembly bolts. Attach both leg assemblies together using the two stretchers. Use 4"-long by ³⁄₈"-diameter bolts and washers to secure the base. The 1" hole on the outside of each vertical support will allow you to recess the bolt head, and the 1"-diameter through-hole in the stretcher board D will be used to attach the nuts to the bolts.

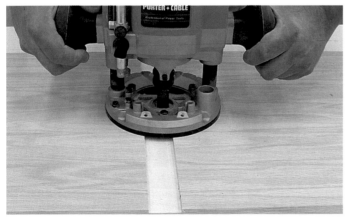

STEP 10 ■ Cut the drawer carcass parts as detailed in the materials list. I am using ³⁄₄"-thick oak veneer plywood to contrast the solid ash.

Apply wood edge tape to all front and top edges of the side boards E. The backboard H requires edge tape on the top and both side edges, as do the front edges of boards F.

Use a router to cut a ¹⁄₄"-deep by 1¹⁄₂"-wide dado in the center inside face of both top and bottom boards for the dividers.

STEP 11 ■ I used three #20 biscuits and glue to attach the carcass sides E to the bottom and top boards F. Dowels or screws and glue can also be used.

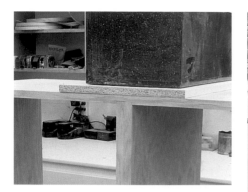

STEP 12 ■ Apply glue to both dadoes and place the dividers G into those dadoes. Use a heavy weight on top of the carcass until the adhesive sets and the dividers are fixed solidly n place.

I'm using two dividers for strength because I don't want the dividers to flex, which may interfere with the drawer·runners if a lot of weight is added to the top board of the carcass. It's possibly overbuilt at this point, but I'd rather have more support than needed instead of just enough.

STEP 13 ■ The backboard H is attached with #20 biscuits and glue. Clamp it in place until the adhesive sets up.

STEP 14 ■ Put the drawer carcass in the bench frame. Rest the bottom board on both stretchers, aligning the backboard with the outside face of the back stretcher. Use 1½" PB screws to secure the carcass to the bench frame. Do not use glue, so it can be removed if the bench must be moved.

STEP 15 ■ I'm installing drawers on both sides of the carcass. One side will have three drawers and the other side two.

Calculating drawer sizes means subtracting 1" from the interior carcass width for most drawer glides. However, it's well worth purchasing your glides at this point to verify the installation instructions.

In a frameless-style cabinet, such as this one, drawer height is found by following a few simple rules. Each drawer box should have 1" clearance above and below. That required space means there will be a 2" space between drawer boxes. The interior space is 18½" high, meaning on a two-drawer bank we must subtract 4" from that height (1" above and below each drawer box for purposes of calculating drawer height), and divide the result by two. The drawer height for the two-drawer bank will be 18½" minus 4" divided by 2, or 7¼" high.

The same calculations apply to the three-drawer bank. The drawer boxes will be 18½" minus 6" divided by 3, or approximately 4⅛" high, to provide the correct clearance.

Cut all the drawer parts to size as detailed in the materials list. These boxes will be constructed using ½" baltic birch plywood.

STEP 16 ■ Each drawer box side J and M will need a rabbet cut ½" wide by ¼" deep on each inside face at both ends. The back and front boards will fit into these rabbets. Use a router table or table saw to make the cuts.

STEP 17 ■ Join the drawer box sides to the back and front boards using glue and 1" brad nails. The nails will hold the joint until the glue dries. Glue and nail the bottom boards to the drawer box frames.

STEP 18 ■ Attach drawer runners to each box. I am using ³/₄-extension glides, but full-extension glides (silver in the photo) can also be used if you require full access to the drawer. The full-extension models are two to three times more expensive than the ³/₄-extension type, but worth the extra cost if you need to fully access the drawer box.

Attach the runners using ¹/₂" screws and follow the manufacturer's instructions.

STEP 19 ■ Mount the cabinet runners using a level line as a guide, or with a drawer glide-mounting jig.

Install one glide at the bottom of each cabinet section, and one 8" above the bottom board in the two-drawer cabinet. The three-drawer section has one set of runners at the bottom, one at 7" above the bottom board, and the top runner set 14" above the bottom.

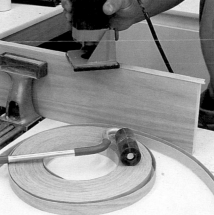

STEP 20 ■ The drawer faces Q, R and S are made using ³/₄"-thick veneer plywood. All four edges of each drawer face have wood veneer tape applied.

STEP 21 ■ Here's an easy way to accurately locate drawer faces. First, drill the handle hole (or holes) in the drawer face, not through the drawer box at this point. Position the drawer face against the cabinet with the drawer box in place. Once located, drive a wood screw through the handle hole and into the drawer box until the face is secure. Next, open the drawer and drive 1" screws through the back of the drawer box front board, into the drawer face. Finally, remove the screws from the handle holes, drill holes completely through the box and install the handles or knobs.

STEP 22 ■ My benchtop T is constructed using six 5¹/₂"-wide boards that are 1¹/₂" thick. The boards are left longer than 72" and will be trimmed to size once the top is sanded. Thick boards can be joined with a double-biscuit technique that's shown in the photo.

STEP 23 ▪ To prepare rough boards for joining, flatten one face on a jointer.

STEP 24 ▪ Next, press the flat face against the jointer fence and mill one edge at 90° to the prepared face.

STEP 25 ▪ Cut the remaining rough edge parallel to the jointed edge, and at 90° to the prepared face, on a table saw. Hold the jointed edge of the board tight to the saw fence and the prepared face flat on the saw table.

STEP 26 ▪ Use a planer to dress the rough face parallel to the prepared face. The board is now ready to be joined to other boards.

STEP 27 ▪ Join the boards with clamps on the top and bottom face as shown. This over-and-under technique will help to ensure that your top will set up flat. Tighten the clamps until you see just a little of the glue squeeze out. Clamps set too tight will squeeze out a lot of glue, starving the joint and possibly making it fail.

STEP 28 ▪ Complete the top by scraping off the excess glue and sanding smooth. Trim to the required 30"-wide by 72"-long size. Turn the top facedown on the floor. Set the leg and carcass assembly upside down on the bottom face of the top so it's equally spaced side to side and front to back. Drill small pilot holes through the upper horizontal support and into the top. One hole at the end of each support is required.

STEP 29 ■ Drill 1"-diameter holes, 1" deep, in the bottom face of the top using the small drill holes from the previous step as a guide. Cut and install four 2½"-long by 1"-diameter dowels in the holes using glue.

Drill 1"-diameter holes completely through the upper horizontal supports using the pilot holes as a guide. Once the adhesive sets, put the top on the base assembly with the dowels set into the four holes. You may need to widen the diameter of the horizontal support holes with sandpaper to install the top.

STEP 30 ■ My front vise is a single-screw model made by Veritas Tools, available from Lee Valley Tools. I followed the installation instructions and added two 1½"-thick wood jaws.

construction NOTES

I drilled ¾"-diameter holes in my benchtop to accommodate round bench dogs. Both vise jaws also had ¾"-diameter holes drilled for the round dogs. These bench dogs can be used with either vise to clamp flat boards that need to be sanded or planed.

The size of this bench, the number of drawers in the storage carcass, the height and the accessory equipment can all be modified to suit your requirements. My bench is 36" high, but that may not be suitable for everyone. If this plan isn't right for you, change the dimensions.

Hardwood is an excellent choice for any workbench. A bench will be around for many years, and may be passed to future generations of woodworkers, so use the best quality hardwood you can afford.

I finished my bench with three coats of oil-based polyurethane that is commonly used on hardwood floors. I gave the top a good coat of hard paste wax to further protect the surface from liquids and adhesive spills.

This is a great project. I hope you'll enjoy your new workbench as much as I enjoy mine.

STEP 31 ■ The end vise I used is also made by Veritas and is a twin-screw model. When using large end vises on this bench, be sure the moving mechanics of the vise clear the bench supports. I used 7¼"-high wood jaws, centering the screws 3" up from the bottom edge of the boards, so both screws would clear the upper horizontal supports.

Power Miter Saw Station

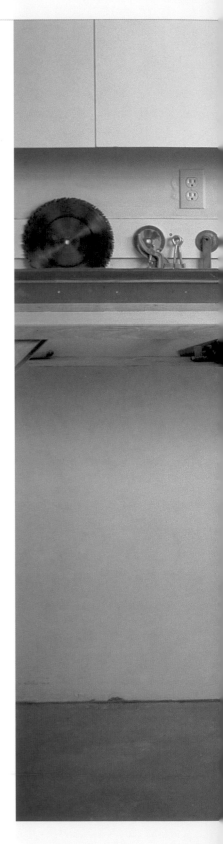

I wanted to meet a number of requirements when I designed my ultimate power miter saw station.

First, the station tower had to be wide enough so I could tuck a large garbage pail inside. It also had to have easy access so I could clear and throw away scraps of wood. I sometimes get lazy and forget to remove the small scraps of wood after cutting. These pieces can contact the blade on the next cut and shoot out of the saw like a wild bullet. I have seen too many close calls using this saw, so this design feature was high on my list.

I also wanted the station fences or "wings" on my station to be high enough so I could use the floor space; I will be storing rolling workstations under the saw fences. My table height is 42" off the ground and the fences are about 2½" higher.

The station tower has a drawer to store wrenches, instruction books and any other saw accessories. I usually spend time searching the shop for these items,

so I promised myself they would have a place in the station.

I was tired of using poorly designed stop blocks that could be used only for material cuts starting at 6" or more. Why couldn't a zero stop be made? I think that need was met with my stop-block system.

Finally, the "wings" had to be strong because they would be 4' to 8' long without a center support. I used hardwood and steel to edge the sheet material and make the stop-block system. The fences are extremely strong and will not deflect under heavy loads.

I used melamine particleboard (PB) for my sheet material and hardwood trim to absorb the bumps and hits during heavy use. I decided to install adjustable plastic cabinet legs so I could level the fences.

This power miter saw station is perfect for my work. It has met all my needs and is a pleasure to use. I'm sure it will be a useful addition to your shop, as well.

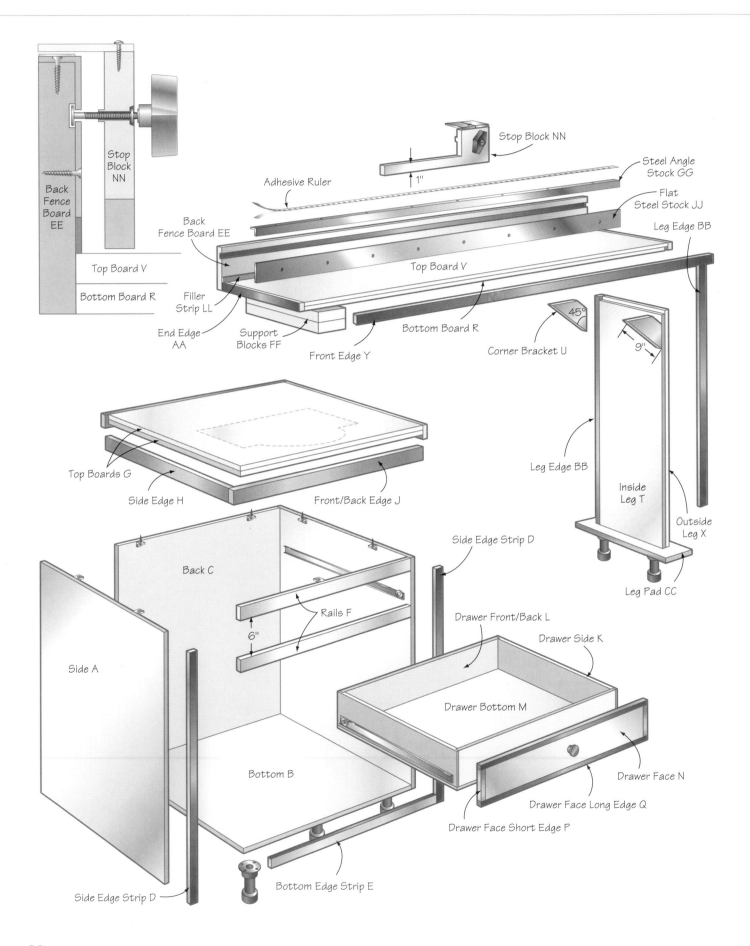

Stop Block NN

Back Fence Board EE

Stop Block NN

Top Board V

Bottom Board R

Adhesive Ruler

Back Fence Board EE

Filler Strip LL

End Edge AA

Support Blocks FF

Front Edge Y

1"

Steel Angle Stock GG

Flat Steel Stock JJ

Leg Edge BB

Top Board V

Bottom Board R

Corner Bracket U

45°

9"

Leg Edge BB

Inside Leg T

Outside Leg X

Leg Pad CC

Top Boards G

Side Edge H

Front/Back Edge J

Side Edge Strip D

Back C

Rails F

6"

Drawer Front/Back L

Drawer Side K

Side A

Drawer Bottom M

Drawer Face N

Bottom B

Drawer Face Long Edge Q

Drawer Face Short Edge P

Side Edge Strip D

Bottom Edge Strip E

materials list ▪ **INCHES**

TOWER

REFERENCE	QUANTITY	PART	STOCK	THICKNESS	WIDTH	LENGTH	COMMENTS
A	2	sides	melamine PB	$5/8$	24	36	
B	1	bottom	melamine PB	$5/8$	26	24	
C	1	back	melamine PB	$5/8$	26	$35^3/8$	
D	2	side edge strips	solid hardwood	$1/4$	$5/8$	36	
E	1	bottom edge strip	solid hardwood	$1/4$	$5/8$	26	
F	2	rails	solid hardwood	$1/4$	$1^1/2$	26	
G	2	top boards	melamine PB	$5/8$	$25^1/4$	$30^1/2$	
H	2	side edges	solid hardwood	$1/4$	$1^1/2$	$25^1/4$	
J	2	front & back edges	solid hardwood	$1/4$	$1^1/2$	32	
K	2	drawer sides	melamine PB	$5/8$	$4^3/8$	22	
L	2	drawer front & back	melamine PB	$5/8$	$4^3/8$	$23^3/4$	
M	1	drawer bottom	melamine PB	$5/8$	22	25	
N	1	drawer face	melamine PB	$5/8$	$6^1/2$	$26^1/2$	
P	2	drawer face edges	solid hardwood	$1/4$	$5/8$	$6^1/2$	
Q	2	drawer face edges	solid hardwood	$1/4$	$5/8$	27	

FENCE WINGS

REFERENCE	QUANTITY	PART	STOCK	THICKNESS	WIDTH	LENGTH	COMMENTS
R	1	bottom board	melamine PB	$5/8$	7	$71^3/8$	
S	1	bottom board	melamine PB	$5/8$	7	$47^3/8$	
T	2	inside legs	melamine PB	$5/8$	7	$38^7/8$	
U	4	corner brackets	solid hardwood	$3/4$	$3^1/2$	9	
V	1	top board	melamine PB	$5/8$	7	72	
W	1	top board	melamine PB	$5/8$	7	48	
X	2	outside legs	melamine PB	$5/8$	7	$39^1/2$	
Y	1	front edge	solid hardwood	$3/4$	$1^1/4$	$73^1/2$	
Z	1	front edge	solid hardwood	$3/4$	$1^1/4$	$49^1/2$	
AA	4	end edges	solid hardwood	$3/4$	$1^1/4$	7	
BB	4	leg edges	solid hardwood	$3/4$	$1^1/4$	$38^7/8$	
CC	2	leg pads	solid hardwood	$3/4$	$3^1/2$	$8^1/2$	
DD	1	back fence board	solid hardwood	$3/4$	$5^1/4$	$49^1/2$	
EE	1	back fence board	solid hardwood	$3/4$	$5^1/4$	$73^1/2$	
FF	2	support blocks	solid hardwood	$1^1/2$	$2^{11}/16$	6	
GG	1	angle stock	steel	$1/8$	1×1	72	
HH	1	angle stock	steel	$1/8$	1×1	48	
JJ	1	flat stock	steel	$1/8$	2	72	
KK	1	flat stock	steel	$1/8$	2	48	
LL	1	filler strip	solid hardwood	$1/8$	$3/4$	72	
MM	1	filler strip	solid hardwood	$1/8$	$3/4$	48	
NN	2	stop blocks	solid hardwood	$3/4$	$3^7/8$	14	

HARDWARE

10 Adjustable plastic cabinet legs

1 – 22" Drawer glide set

7 Metal right-angle brackets

2 Metal self-sticking measuring tapes

1 – $5/16$"-Diameter closet bolt set

2 Stop-block handles

1 Drawer handle

2 – 2" x 3" Plastic or Plexiglass

Metal washers

White iron-on edge tape

Screw cover caps

Screws as detailed

Glue

Wood plugs

2" PB screws

Biscuits or confirmat screws

$5/8$" Screws

Brad nails

Wood putty

1" Screws

3" Screws

Pan head screws and washers

materials list ▪ **MILLIMETERS**

TOWER

REFERENCE	QUANTITY	PART	STOCK	THICKNESS	WIDTH	LENGTH	COMMENTS
A	2	sides	melamine PB	16	610	914	
B	1	bottom	melamine PB	16	660	610	
C	1	back	melamine PB	16	660	899	
D	2	side edge strips	solid hardwood	6	16	914	
E	1	bottom edge strip	solid hardwood	6	16	660	
F	2	rails	solid hardwood	6	38	660	
G	2	top boards	melamine PB	16	641	775	
H	2	side edges	solid hardwood	6	38	641	
J	2	front & back edges	solid hardwood	6	38	813	
K	2	drawer sides	melamine PB	16	112	559	
L	2	drawer front & back	melamine PB	16	112	603	
M	1	drawer bottom	melamine PB	16	559	635	
N	1	drawer face	melamine PB	16	165	673	
P	2	drawer face edges	solid hardwood	6	16	165	
Q	2	drawer face edges	solid hardwood	6	16	686	

FENCE WINGS

REFERENCE	QUANTITY	PART	STOCK	THICKNESS	WIDTH	LENGTH	COMMENTS
R	1	bottom board	melamine PB	16	178	1813	
S	1	bottom board	melamine PB	16	178	1204	
T	2	inside legs	melamine PB	16	178	987	
U	4	corner brackets	solid hardwood	19	89	229	
V	1	top board	melamine PB	16	178	1829	
W	1	top board	melamine PB	16	178	1219	
X	2	outside legs	melamine PB	16	178	1004	
Y	1	front edge	solid hardwood	19	31	1867	
Z	1	front edge	solid hardwood	19	31	1258	
AA	4	end edges	solid hardwood	19	31	178	
BB	4	leg edges	solid hardwood	19	31	987	
CC	2	leg pads	solid hardwood	19	89	216	
DD	1	back fence board	solid hardwood	19	133	1258	
EE	1	back fence board	solid hardwood	19	133	1867	
FF	2	support blocks	solid hardwood	38	69	152	
GG	1	angle stock	steel	3	25 x 25	1829	
HH	1	angle stock	steel	3	25 x 25	1219	
JJ	1	flat stock	steel	3	51	1829	
KK	1	flat stock	steel	3	51	1219	
LL	1	filler strip	solid hardwood	3	19	1829	
MM	1	filler strip	solid hardwood	3	19	1219	
NN	2	stop blocks	solid hardwood	19	98	356	

HARDWARE

10 Adjustable plastic cabinet legs

1 – 559mm Drawer glide set

7 Metal right-angle brackets

2 Metal self-sticking measuring tapes

1 – 8mm-Diameter closet bolt set

2 Stop-block handles

1 Drawer handle

2 – 51mm x 76mm Plastic or Plexiglass

Metal washers

White iron-on edge tape

Screw cover caps

Screws as detailed

Glue

Wood plugs

51mm PB screws

Biscuits or confirmat screws

16mm Screws

Brad nails

Wood putty

25mm Screws

76mm Screws

Pan head screws and washers

BUILDING THE POWER MITER SAW STATION

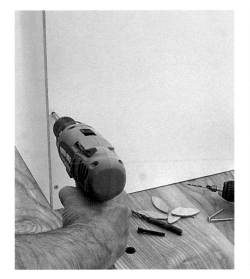

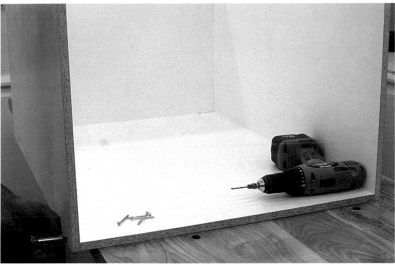

STEP 1 ■ Cut the two sides A and bottom board B as detailed in the materials list. The joinery can be PB screws (on the right in the photo), biscuits (center) or confirmat screws (left). The confirmat screws are European-designed fasteners that are used to assemble melamine PB cabinetry. They are high-quality fasteners, but they do require a special step drill and accurate placement. The drill bits are expensive and brittle. The PB screws are designed to join this material, and the heads can be hidden with plastic cover caps.

I am using 2" PB screws placed 6" apart along the joint. Small white caps or white adhesive covers are available at woodworking and home stores.

STEP 2 ■ The inset backboard C is joined to the sides and bottom board with 2" PB screws. The back face of the backboard is flush with the back edges of the side and bottom boards.

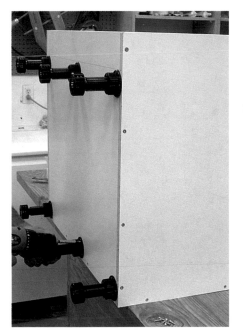

STEP 4 ■ The cabinet edges could suffer a few knocks and bumps, so I installed hardwood edge strips D and E on the bottom and two side panels. Use glue and brad nails to secure the strips of wood. Fill the nail holes with wood putty and sand the strips smooth.

STEP 3 ■ I'm installing six adjustable plastic legs on my tower cabinet. The front legs are set back 3" and secured with four ⅝" screws. Position the flanges of the front and rear outside legs under the edges of the side boards. The load will be transferred directly to the sides, through the legs and onto the floor.

You can build and install a 4"-high base frame made with solid lumber or sheet material if there isn't a danger of liquid spills or water leaks on your shop floor. If water is an issue, or your shop floor isn't level, adjustable cabinet legs are the perfect solution.

Shop Tip

You can avoid splitting panels by keeping screws 1" away from any board end when joining sheet goods. Always drill a pilot hole for the screws to ensure maximum hold.

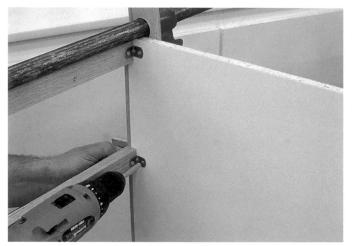

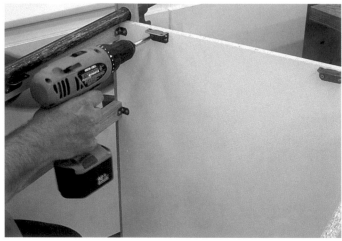

STEP 5 ■ Install the two hardwood rails F, one at the top of the cabinet and the other below it, leaving a 6" space between the rails for a drawer. Secure the rails with right-angle brackets and ⅝" screws, or use pocket holes if you have a jig. Apply a little glue on the front edges to secure the rails to the side wood strips. Clamp until the adhesive cures.

STEP 6 ■ Install seven right-angle brackets using ⅝" screws. One is located in the middle of the top rail and two on each of the back and side boards. These brackets will be used to secure the cabinet top.

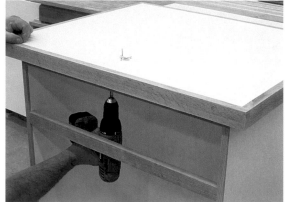

STEP 8 ■ Attach the banded top to the cabinet using 1" screws through the right-angle brackets previously installed. The top overhangs the back by ¾" and by 2⅜" on each side.

STEP 7 ■ The cabinet top G is 32" wide by 26¾" deep overall. It is made with two layers of ⅝"-thick melamine PB, and joined with 1" screws from the underside. A ¾"-thick by 1½"-wide hardwood band, H and J, is applied to all four edges. Use glue and 2" screws in a ⅜" counterbored hole and fill the holes with wood plugs. You can also use biscuits (plate joinery) if you prefer that method.

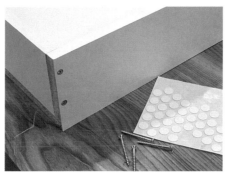

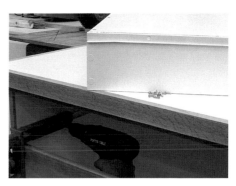

STEP 9 ▪ Drawer boxes are commonly 1" less in height and width when using most ³⁄₄-extension drawer glide sets. This rule is also applied to most full-extension drawer glide sets. However, read the installation instructions with your hardware before cutting the drawer box parts.

Cut the drawer box parts K through M and apply iron-on edge tape to the upper edges of the side, back and front boards. The side edges of the bottom board also require edge tape.

STEP 10 ▪ Join the sides to the back and front boards using 2" PB screws. The bottom board is also installed using 2" screws about 8" apart. Cut the bottom board square and it will ensure that your drawer box is square. The box should be 5" high by 25" wide by 22" deep. The screw heads can be covered with plastic caps or white stick-on covers. Refer to chapter one for more details.

STEP 11 ▪ Mount the drawer glide runners on the cabinet sides, attach the two drawer runners to the box using ⁵⁄₈" screws and test fit your drawer. The cabinet runners can be installed using a straight line made with a carpenter's square, or a drawer glide-mounting jig.

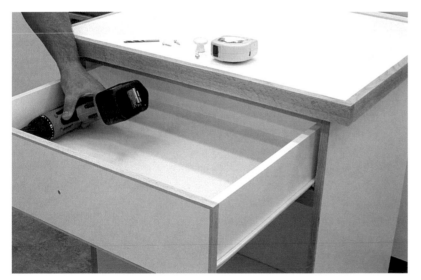

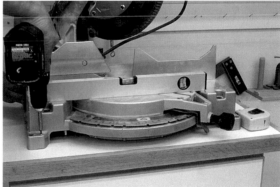

STEP 12 ▪ The finished size of the drawer face is 7" high by 27" wide. I made my drawer face with ⁵⁄₈"-thick melamine PB and ¼"-thick by ⁵⁄₈"-wide hardwood strips on all four edges. The strips were installed with glue and brad nails. To ensure perfect drawer-face alignment, drill the handle or knob holes in the drawer face only. Put the drawer box in the cabinet, hold the drawer face in its correct position, and drive screws through the holes securing it to the drawer box. Then carefully open the drawer and secure the face by driving 1" screws through the drawer box front board into the back of the drawer face. Remove the screw (or screws) in the handle holes and drill through the drawer box. Finally, install the handle to complete the installation.

STEP 13 ▪ Place the tower section where it will be used in your shop and level the cabinet front to back and side to side. Center the miter saw on the top and secure it with screws or bolts. It's difficult to generalize on methods to secure your saw because so many models are available. However, once you have it installed trace an outline on the top with a permanent marker. If the saw has to be removed from the station, it can easily be returned to the same position using the trace lines.

BUILDING THE FENCE PLATFORMS

STEP 14 ■ The right-side fence platform on my station will be 6' long, and the left side will be 4' long. Both will be built with 7"-wide melamine PB and edged with ³⁄₄" hardwood that's 1¹⁄₄" wide so it will cover the double-thickness melamine PB pieces. The lengths of these fence platforms are determined by the amount of space you have available and the type of cutting you do in your shop. Change the lengths of the horizontal boards to suit your shop.

Cut the inside legs T and bottom boards R and S to size. Attach the horizontal bottom shelves to the inside leg top ends using 2" PB screws. Cut the four brackets U and attach two at each corner using 2" screws.

STEP 15 ■ Cut the two top boards V and W, as well as the two outside legs X, to size. Attach the boards as shown in the drawing, using 1" screws from the underside of the bottom top board and back side of the inside leg board. The photo shows proper placement of the boards with the fence assembly's top board resting upside down on the workbench. Two screws, 8" apart and placed in 1" from the edges, will create a solid melamine "sandwich." Hide the screw heads on the legs with plastic caps or stickers.

STEP 16 ■ All the exposed edges, with the exception of the two back edges on the horizontal platforms, are banded with ³⁄₄"-thick by 1¹⁄₄"-wide hardwood. Use glue and screws, in counterbored holes, to attach the hardwood to the front and ends of both platforms, as well as the back and front edges of the legs. Fill the screw head holes with wood plugs.

STEP 17 ■ The size of the leg pad CC will depend on the style of leg you install. My legs require a wide base so I attached a 3¹⁄₂"-wide pad with screws and glue. The legs are secured with four ⁵⁄₈" screws.

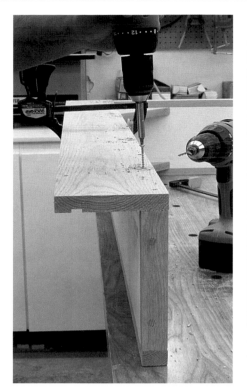

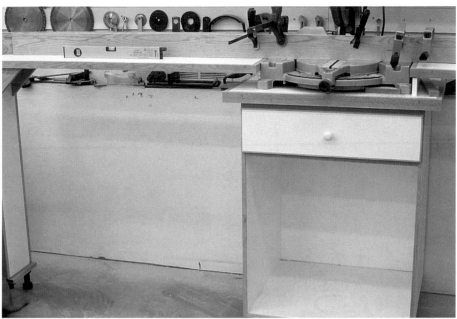

STEP 18 ■ The back fence boards must be cut and grooved before being attached. The groove is ¹/₂" wide by ¹/₈" deep and is located ³/₄" down from the top edge of each fence board. Attach the fence boards DD and EE with glue and 2" screws. The boards are installed with the groove at the top and facing inward toward the platform. The bottom of each fence board is flush with the bottom face of the lower melamine fence platform boards R and S.

STEP 19 ■ Clamp a long straightedge across the saw bed. Level each fence platform by blocking the end that rests on the tower tabletop and adjusting the legs at the ends. The fence platforms must be flush with the saw platform. Set the face of the platform fences ¹/₈" behind the saw fence because we will be installing ¹/₈"-thick steel on the fence.

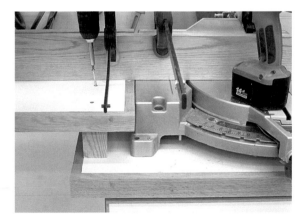

STEP 20 ■ Cut two support blocks FF (the block thickness I needed to match my saw's platform was 2¹¹/₁₆") and attach them to the tower tabletop with screws driven from the underside of that top. Use 3" screws to secure the platforms to each block, making certain the fence platforms are level with the saw's platform.

Shop Tip

Construct or buy a wall bracket if you are concerned about bumping the platforms with heavy lumber. The platforms are solid and stable, but you may want extra support, so attach a bracket between the legs and a wall. The miter station tower can also be anchored to the wall for extra stability, however, the tower and fence platforms are rigid and will remain aligned under normal usage.

STEP 21 ■ The next step is to build a stop-block system. First, drill and attach ¹/₈"-thick steel angle stock parts GG and HH on the top of each platform fence board. Steel angle and flat stock is available at most hardware and home stores. The steel angle stock is ⁷/₈" wide on the inside face and will rest ¹/₈" lower than the top of the fence groove. Be sure to countersink the screw heads so the adhesive steel ruler will lay flat on top of the angle stock.

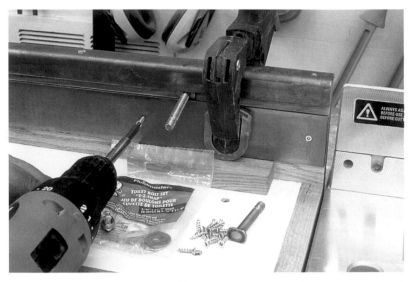

STEP 22 ■ Drill and countersink the ⅛"-thick by 2"-wide steel flat stock pieces JJ and KK. The holes should be about 6" apart and countersunk so the screw heads are below the stock's surface. Attach the flat steel to the back fence boards using ⅝" screws.

The bolts that will be used for the stop assemblies are a toilet or closet bolt set; they are ⁵⁄₁₆"-diameter bolts with large, flat oval heads. Clamp the flat steel below the angle stock with a bolt in the groove. The bolts should move freely, but you shouldn't be able to pull them out.

STEP 23 ■ Once the steel pieces have been installed and the bolts are moving freely along the length of each track, cut and install filler strips LL and MM. These strips will make the fence flush from top to bottom. Use glue and brad nails to secure the strips.

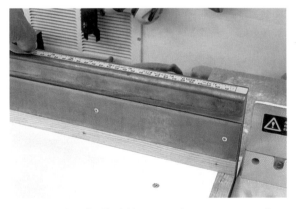

STEP 24 ■ Install self-sticking measuring tapes on top of each angle iron. You'll need left-to-right and right-to-left reading tapes. The zero mark on each ruler should align with the end of each angle iron closest to the miter saw.

STEP 25 ■ Cut stop-block boards NN as shown in the materials list. They will be trimmed to size on the miter station. Set the table saw fence for a ⅝"-thick cut with the blade 1" high. Run both boards through the saw, on edge. Reset the blade 2½" high and run both boards through the saw once again after flipping them. The result will be a ⅛"-thick by ¼"-wide tenon on the back face of each board. The tenon will slide in the space between both pieces of steel and stabilize the stop block.

STEP 26 ■ Cut the stop-block boards on a band saw or with a jigsaw, as shown. The first 3" of the board should be full height and the remainder 1" high. Remember that you'll need a right and left stop-block assembly, so pay close attention to how the cut lines are laid out on each board.

I decided to use steel for these long fence platforms because I didn't want any deflection, and the result was impressive. Both fence systems are stable and rigid.

The fence platforms are high enough so I can store other workstations underneath, which is a real bonus in any shop. I used melamine PB for the field and oak hardwood for the edges; however, any sheet material and wood banding can be used. The smooth surface of the melamine makes it easy to slide the boards being cut, but materials such as medium-density fiberboard will serve the same purpose.

The dimensions of the tower can be changed if you find the height unsuitable. My tower interior width was designed to hold a large plastic pail for scraps, but it can be narrower if you don't need a scrap pail. My platform is wide because my 12" miter saw has a large bed. Smaller saws are common, so design your tower top to hold the saw you own. I don't think there are much wider miter saws on the market, but it's well worth taking the time to measure your saw before building the tower.

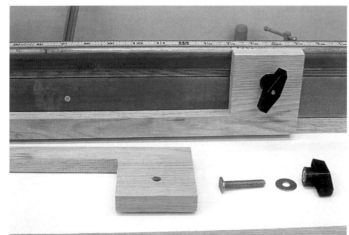

STEP 27 ■ Drill a ³⁄₈"-diameter hole through the middle of each tenon on both stop blocks. The holes should be centered on the width of the full-height portion of each block. Use a closet bolt and washer with a suitable knob to attach each block. I found the knobs at my local hardware store with a thread pattern that matched the closet bolt set. Most woodworking stores also carry these knobs in many styles.

You can include many other features in your design. For example, a rack could be attached to the outside face of the side boards to hold saw blades. Or the drawer could be divided with partitions for various tools and documents that are needed for your saw. I also considered adding another cabinet beside the tower with adjustable shelves for storing small cutoffs that can be used for other projects.

Shop Tip

You can use aluminum stock, but steel is about one-half the cost and is much stronger. The same fence system can also be built using an aluminum T-track set into a groove in the back fence board. I've opted for steel in this case because it strengthens the fence platforms.

If you don't have access to adjustable legs, or prefer a solid base, you can construct one with 2x4 material or plywood. The steel, closet bolts and knobs are common hardware items and should be readily available at your local hardware store.

STEP 28 ■ The stop-block position is determined by a clear plastic indicator screwed to the top of each stop block. Clear plastic or Plexiglass is available at craft and plastic supply stores.

Cut two pieces each 2" wide by 3" long. Scribe a fine line in the plastic with an awl or other sharp tool. Use a permanent marker to fill the scratch with ink. Attach the indicator to the stop block with pan head screws and washers in oval-shaped holes that will allow side-to-side adjustment. Align the mark on the plastic indicator to zero on the tape measure and trim the tongue on the stop block with your miter saw. That's your zero measurement for each block, and if you need to fine-tune the adjustment, loosen the screws and move the plastic indicator.

project **FOUR**

Multifunction Power Tool Cabinet

A power tool stand is a great addition to any workshop; however, if you have limited space, need to move the tools out of the way for your car or don't use certain tools on a regular basis, a dedicated power tool station is not much use. I think you'll find this tool cabinet answers all those needs.

This versatile tool cabinet has a removable platform that locks securely into place in less than a minute. It can be used with dozens of power tools that are secured to individual mounting boards. The cabinet has four locking wheels, an open shelf for accessories, and a drawer to store all the documentation and extra parts that come with your tools.

The cabinet is built with tough, inexpensive $\frac{5}{8}$" melamine particleboard (PB) and hardwood edging so it will last for years. It can be tucked away in a corner

or stored under the miter saw station wings described in chapter three.

The top and tool platforms are constructed using $\frac{3}{4}$"-thick medium-density fiberboard (MDF), which is another inexpensive sheet material. The drawer is $\frac{5}{8}$" melamine PB and mounted on $\frac{3}{4}$-extension, bottom-mount drawer glides. The cabinet also has enough room to store a second power tool on its mounting platform, in the bottom section.

This has been one of the most valuable cabinets I've built for my shop. Moving the power tools to my work area, with all the accessories on board where I can quickly locate them, is a real benefit, and I'm enjoying my work even more. I was so pleased with this mobile tool cabinet that I built two and may build another in the near future. I hope you'll find it just as useful and build one or two for your shop.

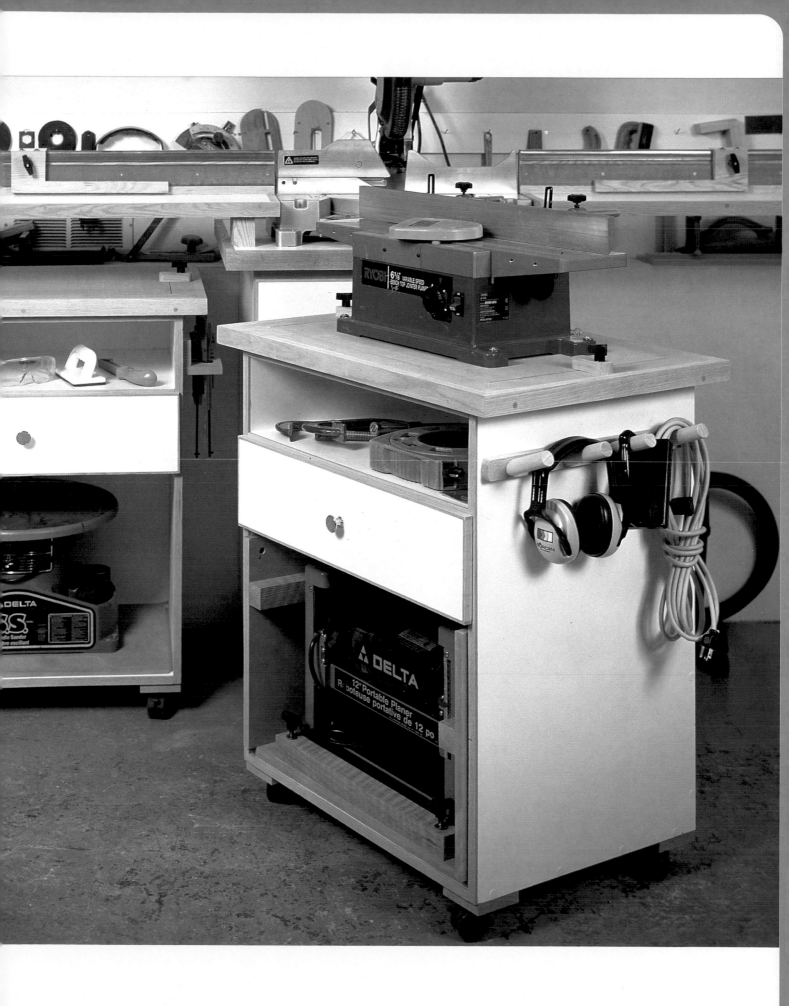

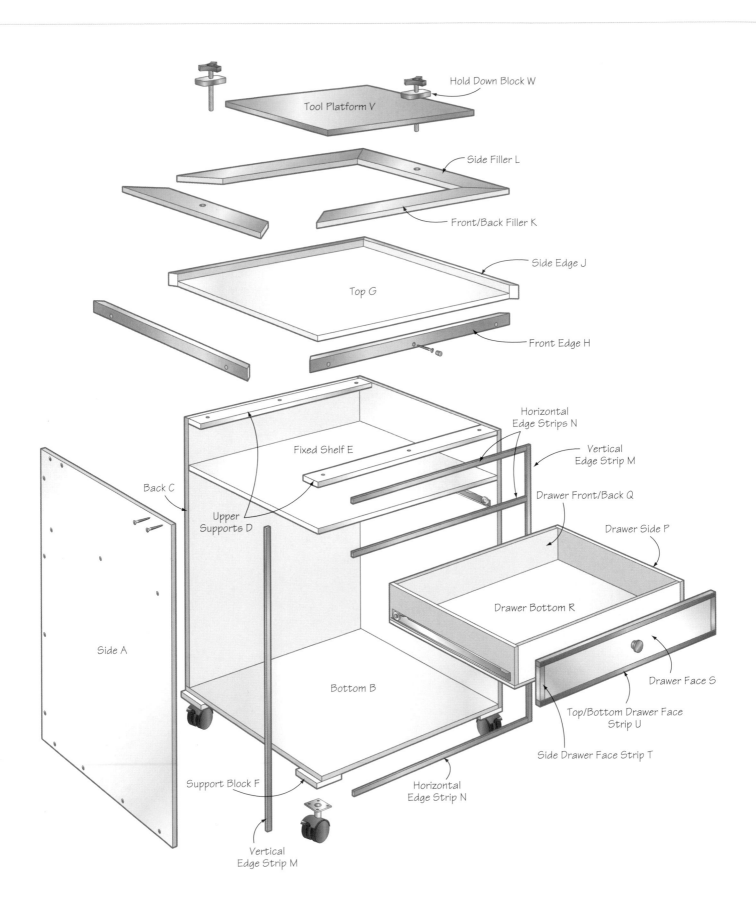

Hold Down Block W

Tool Platform V

Side Filler L

Front/Back Filler K

Side Edge J

Top G

Front Edge H

Horizontal Edge Strips N

Vertical Edge Strip M

Fixed Shelf E

Drawer Front/Back Q

Drawer Side P

Back C

Upper Supports D

Drawer Bottom R

Side A

Drawer Face S

Bottom B

Top/Bottom Drawer Face Strip U

Side Drawer Face Strip T

Support Block F

Horizontal Edge Strip N

Vertical Edge Strip M

materials list ▪ **INCHES**

REFERENCE	QUANTITY	PART	STOCK	THICKNESS	WIDTH	LENGTH	COMMENTS
A	2	sides	melamine PB	$5/8$	20	32	
B	1	bottom	melamine PB	$5/8$	20	26	
C	1	back	melamine PB	$5/8$	26	$31^3/8$	
D	2	upper supports	melamine PB	$5/8$	4	26	
E	1	fixed shelf	melamine PB	$5/8$	$19^3/8$	26	
F	4	support blocks	hardwood	$3/4$	$3^1/2$	$3^1/2$	
G	1	top	melamine PB	$5/8$	21	30	
H	2	front & back edges	hardwood	$3/4$	$1^3/8$	$31^1/2$	angle-cut
J	2	side edges	hardwood	$3/4$	$1^3/8$	$22^1/2$	angle-cut
K	2	front & back top fillers	MDF	$3/4$	$2^1/4$	30	angle-cut
L	2	side fillers	MDF	$3/4$	$2^1/4$	21	angle-cut
M	2	vertical edge strips	hardwood	$1/4$	$5/8$	32	
N	3	horizontal edge strips	hardwood	$1/4$	$5/8$	26	
P	2	drawer sides	melamine PB	$5/8$	$4^3/8$	18	
Q	2	drawer front & back	melamine PB	$5/8$	$4^3/8$	$23^3/4$	
R	1	drawer bottom	melamine PB	$5/8$	18	25	
S	1	drawer face	melamine PB	$5/8$	$6^1/2$	$26^1/2$	
T	2	side drawer face strips	hardwood	$1/4$	$5/8$	$6^1/2$	
U	2	top/bottom drawer face strips	hardwood	$1/4$	$5/8$	27	
V	3	tool platforms	MDF	$3/4$	$16^1/2$	$25^1/2$	
W	2	hold-down blocks	hardwood	$3/4$	$1^1/2$	3	

HARDWARE

4 Locking wheel casters
1 – 18" Drawer glide set
2 Knobs, $1/4$"-diameter thread
2 Hanger bolts, $2^1/2$"-long x $1/4$"-diameter thread
2 – $1/4$" Metal washers
White iron-on edge tape
Screw cover caps
Screws as detailed
Glue
Wood plugs
2" Screws
Biscuits
Dowels
$1^1/4$" Screws
1" Screws
Brad nails
Wood putty
$5/8$" Screws

materials list ▪ **MILLIMETERS**

REFERENCE	QUANTITY	PART	STOCK	THICKNESS	WIDTH	LENGTH	COMMENTS
A	2	sides	melamine PB	16	508	813	
B	1	bottom	melamine PB	16	508	660	
C	1	back	melamine PB	16	660	797	
D	2	upper supports	melamine PB	16	102	660	
E	1	fixed shelf	melamine PB	16	493	660	
F	4	support blocks	hardwood	19	89	89	
G	1	top	melamine PB	16	533	762	
H	2	front & back edges	hardwood	19	35	800	angle-cut
J	2	side edges	hardwood	19	35	572	angle-cut
K	2	front & back top fillers	MDF	19	57	762	angle-cut
L	2	side fillers	MDF	19	57	533	angle-cut
M	2	vertical edge strips	hardwood	6	16	813	
N	3	horizontal edge strips	hardwood	6	16	660	
P	2	drawer sides	melamine PB	16	112	457	
Q	2	drawer front & back	melamine PB	16	112	603	
R	1	drawer bottom	melamine PB	16	457	635	
S	1	drawer face	melamine PB	16	165	673	
T	2	side drawer face strips	hardwood	6	16	165	
U	2	top/bottom drawer face strips	hardwood	6	16	686	
V	3	tool platforms	MDF	19	419	648	
W	2	hold-down blocks	hardwood	19	38	76	

HARDWARE

4 Locking wheel casters
1 – 457mm Drawer glide set
2 Knobs, 6mm-diameter thread
2 Hanger bolts, 64mm-long x 6mm-diameter thread
2 – 6mm Metal washers
White iron-on edge tape
Screw cover caps
Screws as detailed
Glue
Wood plugs
51mm Screws
Biscuits
Dowels
32mm Screws
25mm Screws
Brad nails
Wood putty
16mm Screws

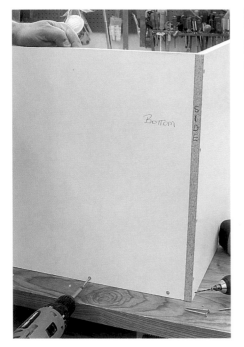

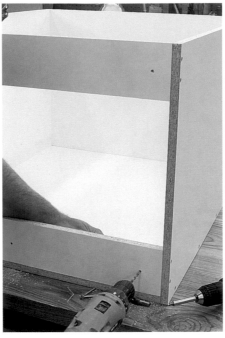

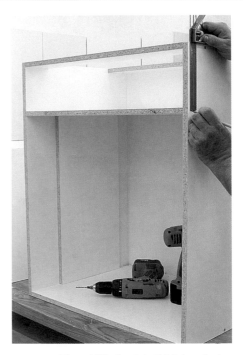

STEP 1 ■ Cut the sides A, bottom B and back C to the sizes listed in the materials list using $\frac{5}{8}$" melamine PB. Attach the sides to the bottom board using 2" PB screws in pilot holes spaced 6" apart. The inset backboard is also attached with screws through the side and bottom boards.

The joinery can be done with PB screws, biscuits or dowels and glue. The screw heads can be covered with plastic or self-adhesive cover caps.

STEP 2 ■ The two upper supports D are added so the cabinet sides remain parallel at the top. They will also be used to secure the top board. Cut the two supports to length, installing the front board flush with the edges of the side panels. Secure the boards with 2" PB screws, placed 1" in from each edge to avoid splitting the boards. Drill through-holes for the screws, which will be used to secure the top.

STEP 3 ■ The middle fixed shelf E is installed 6" below the bottom surface of the upper supports. Holding a shelf accurately in place is difficult, so I've cut two $24\frac{1}{8}$"-high temporary spacers to properly locate the shelf. Use a square to mark the screw position in the center of the fixed shelf's edge on the side and back panels. Drive 2" screws, in pilot holes, through the panels to secure the shelf. Cover the screw heads with caps.

STEP 4 ■ Attach four caster support blocks F on the corners of the cabinet. Position the blocks so the outside edges are flush with the outside edges of the cabinet. Use 2" screws on the outside edges through the blocks and into the back or side boards. The inner edges are secured with $1\frac{1}{4}$" screws into the bottom board.

Shop Tip

Many woodworkers have a sliding table for crosscutting panels; however, it isn't safe to use the fence and another guide device when crosscutting because there's a possibility that the board will bind in the blade and be thrown backwards. Instead you can use the measuring feature on your saw fence by adding a stop block. The panel being cut on a sliding table will leave the block before it completes

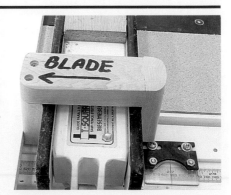

the cut, making the operation safe. Remember to add 1" (with a 1"-thick block) to the fence distance to account for the stop-block thickness.

STEP 5 ■ Mount four locking casters on the blocks using 1¼" screws or lag bolts.

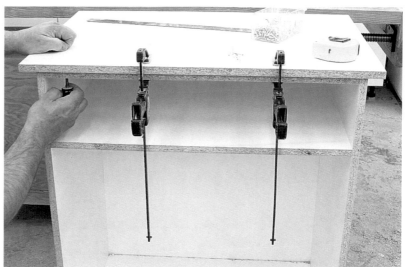

STEP 6 ■ Attach the cabinet top G with an overhang of ½" on the front and back. The sides will have an overhang of 1⅜". Use 1" screws through the upper supports D to secure the top board.

STEP 7 ■ The top board G is banded with ¾"-thick by 1⅜"-high hardwood. The hardwood edge is flush with the bottom face of the top board and ¾" above the top's surface. Cut the corners of the hardwood banding at 45° and secure them with biscuits and glue or, as I'm using, screws and glue. Fill the counterbored holes with wood plugs and sand smooth.

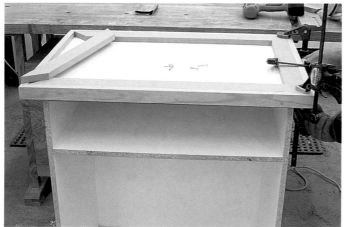

STEP 8 ■ The tabletop fillers K and L are ¾" MDF. One sheet of 4x8 MDF has enough material for six tool platforms as well as the 2¼"-wide filler boards. The corners are joined at 45°, and the fillers are held in place with 1¼" screws from the underside of the tabletop.

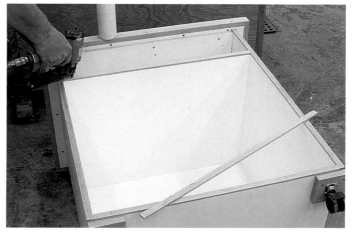

STEP 9 ■ Lay the cabinet on its back and trim the edges with ¼"-thick by ⅝"-wide hardwood strips M and N. Attach the strips with glue and brad nails. Fill the nail holes with wood putty and sand smooth.

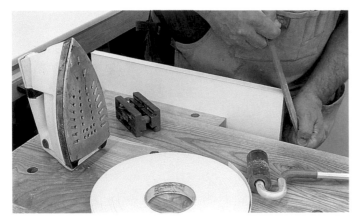

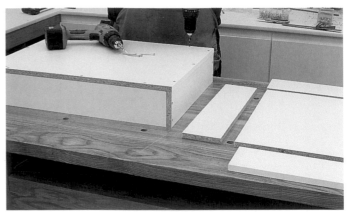

STEP 10 ■ The next step is to build an accessory drawer under the fixed shelf. The drawer box is 5" high by 18" deep and 1" narrower than the inside cabinet width, or 25". It will be installed with bottom-mounted $^3/_4$-extension drawer glides. The drawer box is constructed using $^5/_8$"-thick melamine PB.

Cut the drawer sides P, front and back Q and drawer bottom R. Use iron-on edge tape to cover the top edges of the sides, back and front boards, as well as the side edges of the bottom board.

STEP 11 ■ Attach the drawer box sides to the back and front boards using 2" PB screws in pilot holes. Attach the bottom using 2" PB screws.

STEP 13 ■ The drawer face S is 2" wider and 2" higher than the drawer box, or 27" wide by 7" high. The drawer face is trimmed with $^1/_4$"-thick by $^5/_8$"-wide hardwood strips. To arrive at the final height, cut the melamine PB center $^1/_2$" less in width and height.

Attach the edge strips T and U with glue and brad nails. Fill the holes with wood putty and sand the edges smooth.

STEP 12 ■ Install the drawer glide hardware following the manufacturer's instructions. The cabinet runners are installed with the bottom track 6" below the fixed storage shelf E. Use a carpenter's square to draw a screw-hole reference line or a drawer glide-mounting jig to install the runners with $^5/_8$" screws.

STEP 14 ■ Attach the face to the drawer box using 1" screws through the back side of the drawer box front board. I drill the handle hole (or holes) in my drawer face and drive a screw through that hole to temporarily secure the face board in the proper position. Then I gently open the drawer and install the 1" screws through the back. Once the face is secure, I remove the screw from the handle hole and drill completely through the drawer box to install a knob or handle.

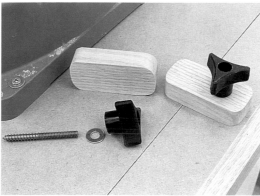

STEP 15 ■ The tool platforms V are $^3/_4$"-thick MDF. I cut three platforms for each of my two mobile tool stations. However, you can make as many as you need to mount your power tools. A platform without a tool can be used as a mobile worktable when needed.

STEP 16 ■ The tool platforms are held in place with a simple lock assembly. Screw a 2$^1/_2$"-long by $^1/_4$"-diameter hanger bolt into the side fillers, 1" back from the inside edge. Cut and round over the corners of a $^3/_4$"-thick by 3"-long piece of hardwood. Drill a $^5/_{16}$"-diameter hole in this hold-down block W, 1" from an end, and slip it over the hanger bolt. Place a metal washer on the bolt and attach a $^1/_4$"-diameter threaded knob. One block on each side will secure the tool platform when the knobs are tightened.

Most of the benchtop power tools in my shop will fit on the 16$^1/_2$"-deep by 25$^1/_2$"-wide platforms; however, the cabinet size should meet your needs. Build it to the dimensions shown in this chapter or change the width, height or depth as needed. If you do alter the platform size, be sure it will fit in the lower section of the cabinet to take advantage of all the storage space.

I used melamine particleboard and medium-density fiberboard, but any sheet material you feel comfortable with will work just as well. I like these materials because they are inexpensive and, in the case of melamine PB, already finished with a tough coating. Both materials can be securely joined using PB screws.

These power tool stations are mobile but can be made stationary by replacing the wheels with a fixed base. They'll work just as well against a wall if you have the space available. I opted for mobile units because they can be tucked away under the wings of my power miter saw station, built in chapter three.

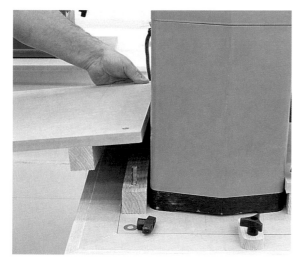

STEP 17 ■ Benchtop power tools, like the planer shown in this photograph, require infeed and outfeed tables. If they were fixed in place, the tool would be larger than the platform's footprint, making storage difficult. You can easily build removable platforms using hanger bolts, spacer cleats and knobs. In this example my feed tables are longer than the factory-supplied models and will provide more support for the material being machined.

STEP 18 ■ Dozens of different tool holders can be attached to the sides of your mobile power tool cabinets. Extension cords, safety equipment and other accessories required when working with different benchtop power tools can be installed.

Power Tool Storage Station

he multifunction power tool cabinets I built in chapter four are great. So great, in fact, that I've mounted a number of my benchtop tools on the interchangeable table inserts. However, I discovered that I needed more storage space for these tools on platforms.

I didn't want a cabinet that took up a lot of valuable space in my shop, so I designed this tall storage station. It uses less than 3' square of shop floor to store a number of power tools. This storage station is the perfect companion to the tool cabinet in chapter four.

The station is built with ⅝"-thick melamine particleboard (PB) and has holes drilled 2" apart for plastic-covered steel shelf pins. The pins can be placed in any of the vertical holes, allowing you to design your own storage arrangement.

You don't have to remove the benchtop tools from their drop-in platforms; they slide right into the storage station on the steel pins. Each platform rests on six shelf pins, so they are well supported.

The tool station can be made with less than two sheets of material, which means it's not expensive to build. The tools mounted to the platforms drop into the multifunction cabinet and you're ready to work. Fast access to tools, compact storage and a reasonable construction cost make this storage station well worth building. It can also be used with shelf boards for other shop tools, even if you don't build the multifunction cabinet in chapter four. Simply cut shelf boards to fit and locate the pins to suit your storage requirements.

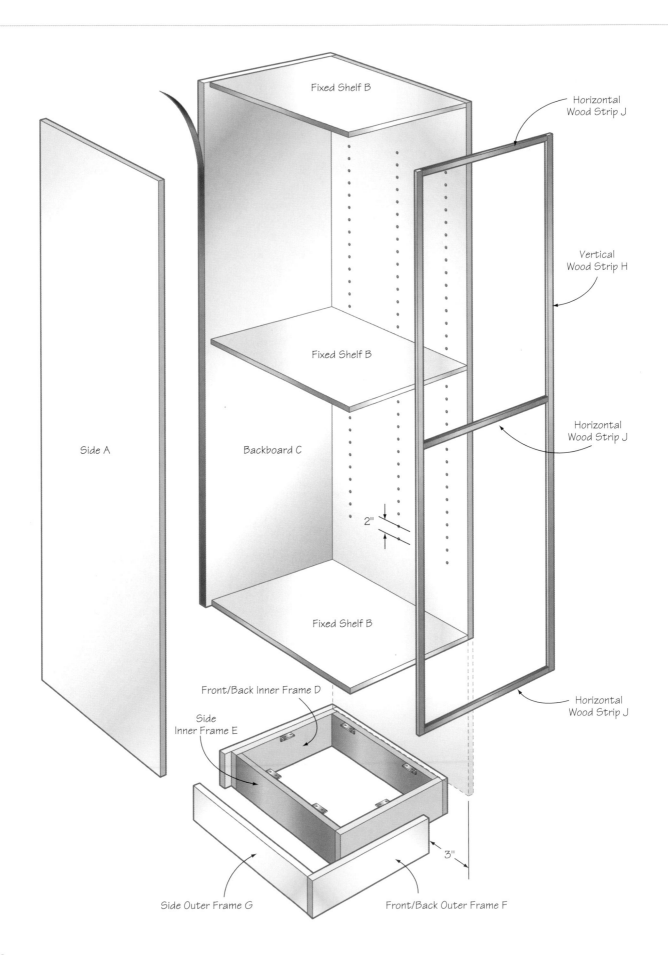

Fixed Shelf B

Horizontal
Wood Strip J

Vertical
Wood Strip H

Fixed Shelf B

Side A

Backboard C

Horizontal
Wood Strip J

2"

Fixed Shelf B

Front/Back Inner Frame D

Side
Inner Frame E

Horizontal
Wood Strip J

3"

Side Outer Frame G

Front/Back Outer Frame F

materials list ▪ **INCHES**

REFERENCE	QUANTITY	PART	STOCK	THICKNESS	WIDTH	LENGTH	COMMENTS
A	2	sides	melamine PB	$5/8$	$25^1/_2$	84	
B	3	fixed shelves	melamine PB	$5/8$	$16^9/_{16}$	$25^1/_2$	
C	1	backboard	melamine PB	$5/8$	$17^{13}/_{16}$	84	
D	2	front & back inner frame	melamine PB	$5/8$	3	$16^9/_{16}$	
E	2	side inner frame	melamine PB	$5/8$	3	20	
F	2	front & back outer frame	melamine PB	$5/8$	3	$17^{13}/_{16}$	
G	2	sides outer frame	melamine PB	$5/8$	3	$21^1/_4$	
H	2	vertical wood strips	solid wood	$1/4$	$5/8$	84	
J	3	horizontal wood strips	solid wood	$1/4$	$5/8$	$16^9/_{16}$	

HARDWARE

6 Metal right-angle brackets

Steel shelf pins as required

2" PB screws

Brad nails

Glue

White screw head cover caps

Iron-on edge tape

1" PB screws

$5/8$" Screws

Wood putty

materials list ▪ **MILLIMETERS**

REFERENCE	QUANTITY	PART	STOCK	THICKNESS	WIDTH	LENGTH	COMMENTS
A	2	sides	melamine PB	16	648	2134	
B	3	fixed shelves	melamine PB	16	420	648	
C	1	backboard	melamine PB	16	453	2134	
D	2	front & back inner frame	melamine PB	16	76	420	
E	2	sides inner frame	melamine PB	16	76	508	
F	2	front & back outer frame	melamine PB	16	76	453	
G	2	sides outer frame	melamine PB	16	76	539	
H	2	vertical wood strips	solid hardwood	6	16	2134	
J	3	horizontal wood strips	solid hardwood	6	16	420	

HARDWARE

6 Metal right-angle brackets

Steel shelf pins as required

51mm PB screws

Brad nails

Glue

White screw head cover caps

Iron-on edge tape

25mm PB screws

16mm Screws

Wood putty

STEP 1 ■ Cut the two sides A and drill holes for the steel shelf pins. The hole diameter should match the shelf pin you decide to use. There are three vertical rows of holes in each side; one is in the center of the panel and the other two are located 1½" in from the front and back edges. Space the holes 2" apart and begin drilling the columns 12" from the top and bottom.

I am using a shop jig made of ⅝"-thick melamine and a wood dowel as a drill depth limiter. The dowel stop is set 1⅛" above the drill end for a ½"-deep hole in the cabinet sides.

STEP 2 ■ The three fixed shelves B are located at the bottom, top and middle of each side panel. Use 2" PB screws in pilot holes to attach the two sides to the shelves. The screw heads can be covered with white cover caps, or you could use biscuits and glue if you don't want fasteners showing. The position of the middle shelf isn't critical as long as it's near the midpoint of the cabinet for side panel support.

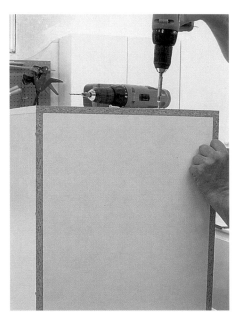

STEP 3 ■ Cover both long edges of the backboard C with melamine iron-on edge tape. Attach the back to the cabinet carcass using 2" PB screws spaced about 8" apart. The carcass will be square if the backboard is cut square. You can ensure a proper fit by aligning one corner of the back with the carcass and securing it with a screw. Next, attach each of the following three corners in order, aligning and fastening each with a screw, then install the remaining screws between the corners.

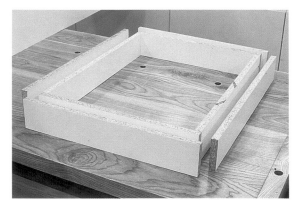

STEP 4 ■ The base frame is built with ⅝"-thick melamine PB. I normally build solid base platforms using two thicknesses of material. The 3"-high pieces of PB are often the waste or cutoffs after the carcass parts are cut, so doubling the base frame thickness is inexpensive insurance.

The inside frame is 16⁹⁄₁₆" wide by 21¼" deep, and the outside frame is 17¹³⁄₁₆" wide by 22½" deep because the frame is set 3" back from the front edge of the cabinet. The base frame will support the cabinet sides and transfer the load to the floor. Apply white edge tape to the outside edges of the back and front boards as these cut ends will be visible.

STEP 5 ■ Build the inner frame using 2" PB screws. The outer frame parts are secured to the inner frame with 1" PB screws through the back faces of the inner frame.

STEP 6 ▪ Attach the base frame to the cabinet using metal right-angle brackets and ⅝" screws.

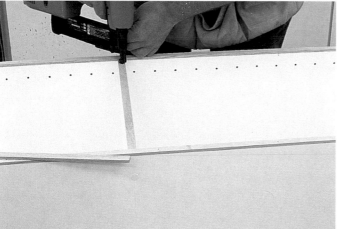

STEP 7 ▪ Glue and nail the wood strips H and J to the front edges of the cabinet sides and fixed shelves. Fill the nail holes with wood putty and sand smooth.

STEP 8 ▪ Use steel or plastic-covered steel shelf pins to properly support the tool platforms.

This project is simple to build and has become a valuable space saver in my shop. I've used melamine PB, but the storage cabinet can be built with any sheet material, such as MDF or plywood.

Plastic adjustable cabinet legs can be used in place of the solid base frame. The legs are often installed when moisture is an issue in the shop. If your shop floor is uneven, plastic adjustable legs may be the obvious choice for your base.

As discussed, the position of the middle shelf isn't critical; however, take note of the benchtop tools you plan to store and secure the shelf close to the middle to maximize tool storage. Three of your benchtop tools on platforms may fit below the fixed shelf if it is positioned at a certain height. Measure the spaces required for your tools and position the shelf accordingly to maximize storage.

If dust is a serious problem in your shop, you might consider installing a door on the cabinet. The door width equals the cabinet's interior width plus 1" when using hidden hinges. The door height is the same as the cabinet side board's height. Using those calculations, you'll need a door that's 17⁹⁄₁₆" wide by 84" high. Drill 35mm-diameter holes, ⅛" from the edge of the door, and install the hinges as detailed in chapter one. Standard-opening hinges, in the 100° to 120° range, cannot be used because the door edge opens into the cabinet's interior space. Use the wide 170° hinges for this application to permit easy installation and removal of the tool platforms.

Mobile Table Saw Center

The first and most important issue you should deal with before starting construction on this Mobile Table Saw Center is the determination of the final table saw height. My saw table is 34" above the floor, which may not be suitable for everyone. The total height is the sum of the wheels, cabinet and benchtop saw heights.

Support your saw at different heights to find one that suits you, then, to determine the cabinet dimensions, subtract the height of the saw and wheels from the total height you've chosen.

Building a mobile table saw center for your benchtop table saw will improve the ease and accuracy of your work. It's well accepted that a good fence and sliding table or crosscut sled are valuable add-ons to any saw. Drawers for storage, a good dust collection system, quick access to accessories as well as the mobility feature combine to make using the saw fun and easy.

This cabinet top should accommodate any benchtop saw, but it's worth measuring yours before you start building the center. The cabinet length addresses a couple of issues. First, it allows you to store tools such as push sticks, hearing protection, miter slides and other often-used accessories in a place where they can be seen and easily accessed. Second, the top supports extended fence tables and protects the guide rail extensions. Finally, the cabinet is long enough for a dust chamber, two large drawers and a storage section with adjustable shelves.

My center will be used in a shop that needs access to a good saw once or twice a month. When the saw isn't needed, simply roll it against a wall or tuck it into an unused corner. If you have a small shop, use a table saw for your woodwork only on an occasional basis or share your garage shop with the family car, this project is for you.

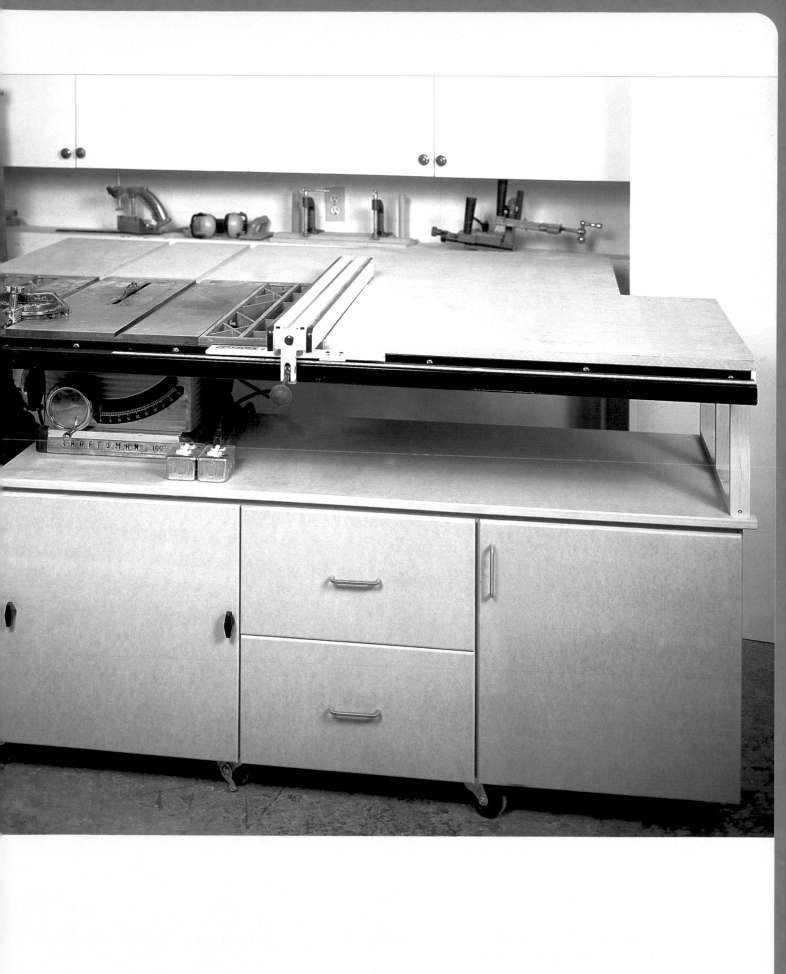

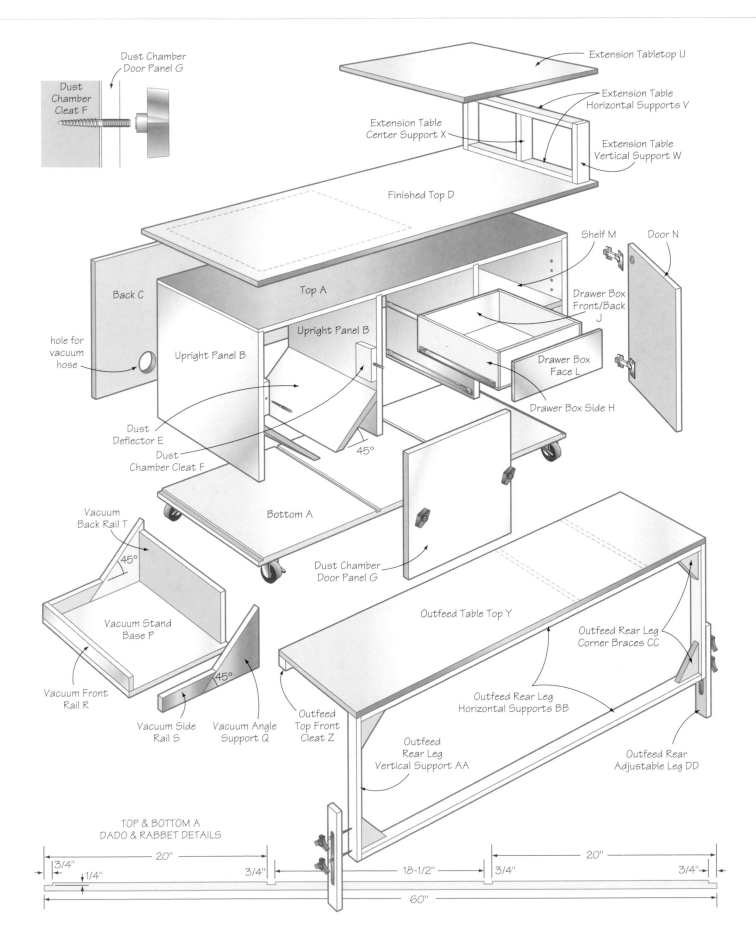

Dust Chamber Door Panel G

Dust Chamber Cleat F

Extension Tabletop U

Extension Table Horizontal Supports V

Extension Table Center Support X

Extension Table Vertical Support W

Finished Top D

Shelf M

Door N

Back C

Top A

Upright Panel B

Drawer Box Front/Back J

hole for vacuum hose

Upright Panel B

Drawer Box Face L

Upright Panel B

Drawer Box Side H

Dust Deflector E

Dust Chamber Cleat F

45°

Bottom A

Dust Chamber Door Panel G

Vacuum Back Rail T

45°

Outfeed Table Top Y

Outfeed Rear Leg Corner Braces CC

Vacuum Stand Base P

Outfeed Rear Leg Horizontal Supports BB

Vacuum Front Rail R

45°

Outfeed Top Front Cleat Z

Outfeed Rear Adjustable Leg DD

Vacuum Side Rail S

Vacuum Angle Support Q

Outfeed Rear Leg Vertical Support AA

TOP & BOTTOM A
DADO & RABBET DETAILS

3/4"

20"

1/4"

3/4"

18-1/2"

3/4"

20"

3/4"

60"

materials list ■ **INCHES**

REFERENCE	QUANTITY	PART	STOCK	THICKNESS	WIDTH	LENGTH	COMMENTS
A	2	top & bottom	MDF	3/4	22$\frac{1}{2}$	60	
B	4	upright panels	MDF	3/4	22$\frac{1}{2}$	16	
C	1	back	MDF	3/4	17	60	
D	1	finished top	MDF	3/4	25	62	
E	2	dust deflectors	MDF	3/4	10	22$\frac{1}{2}$	angle-cut
F	2	dust chamber cleats	MDF	3/4	2	4	
G	1	dust chamber door panel	MDF	3/4	20	16$\frac{1}{2}$	
H	4	drawer box sides	MDF	3/4	5$\frac{1}{4}$	22	
J	4	drawer box fronts & backs	MDF	3/4	5$\frac{1}{4}$	16	
K	2	drawer box bottoms	MDF	3/4	17$\frac{1}{2}$	22	
L	2	drawer box faces	MDF	3/4	8$\frac{3}{16}$	19	
M	1	shelf	MDF	3/4	19$\frac{3}{16}$	22$\frac{3}{8}$	
N	1	door	MDF	3/4	20	16$\frac{1}{2}$	
P	1	vacuum stand base	MDF	3/4	18	23$\frac{1}{4}$	
Q	2	vacuum angle supports	MDF	3/4	11$\frac{1}{4}$	11$\frac{1}{4}$	cut at 45°
R	1	vacuum front rail	MDF	3/4	3	23$\frac{1}{4}$	
S	2	vacuum side rails	MDF	3/4	3	8$\frac{3}{4}$	angle-cut
T	1	vacuum back rail	MDF	3/4	10	21$\frac{3}{4}$	
U	1	extension tabletop	MDF	3/4	27	33	
V	2	ext. horizontal supports	hardwood	3/4	1$\frac{1}{2}$	24	
W	2	ext. vertical supports	hardwood	3/4	1$\frac{1}{2}$	12	
X	1	ext. center support	hardwood	3/4	1$\frac{1}{2}$	10$\frac{1}{2}$	
Y	1	outfeed tabletop	MDF	3/4	27	64	
Z	1	outfeed top front cleat	hardwood	3/4	1$\frac{1}{4}$	64	
AA	2	rear leg vertical supports	hardwood	3/4	1$\frac{1}{2}$	28	
BB	2	rear leg horizontal supports	hardwood	3/4	1$\frac{1}{2}$	62$\frac{1}{2}$	
CC	4	rear leg corner braces	hardwood	3/4	5$\frac{1}{4}$	5$\frac{1}{4}$	angle-cut
DD	2	rear adjustable legs	hardwood	3/4	1$\frac{1}{2}$	16	

HARDWARE

8 Locking wheel casters

2 - 22" Drawer glide sets

Adjustable shelf pins as detailed

2 - 107° Hidden hinges

8 Knobs

8 Hanger bolts, 2"-long x $\frac{1}{4}$"-diameter thread

Door and drawer handles as detailed

Electrical switch, plug and junction boxes

Screws as detailed

Glue

2" PB screws

Biscuits

1$\frac{1}{4}$" Screws

Brad nails

$\frac{5}{8}$" Screws

1$\frac{1}{2}$" Screws

1$\frac{1}{2}$"-Long by $\frac{1}{4}$"-diameter carriage bolts with washers & nuts

T-square fence system

2" Wood screws

REFERENCE	QUANTITY	PART	STOCK	THICKNESS	WIDTH	LENGTH	COMMENTS
A	2	top & bottom	MDF	19	572	1524	
B	4	upright panels	MDF	19	572	406	
C	1	back	MDF	19	432	1524	
D	1	finished top	MDF	19	635	1575	
E	2	dust deflectors	MDF	19	254	572	angle-cut
F	2	dust chamber cleats	MDF	19	51	102	
G	1	dust chamber door panel	MDF	19	508	419	
H	4	drawer box sides	MDF	19	133	559	
J	4	drawer box fronts & backs	MDF	19	133	406	
K	2	drawer box bottoms	MDF	19	445	559	
L	2	drawer box faces	MDF	19	208	483	
M	1	shelf	MDF	19	488	569	
N	1	door	MDF	19	508	419	
P	1	vacuum stand base	MDF	19	457	590	
Q	2	vacuum angle supports	MDF	19	285	285	cut at 45°
R	1	vacuum front rail	MDF	19	76	590	
S	2	vacuum side rails	MDF	19	76	222	angle-cut
T	1	vacuum back rail	MDF	19	254	552	
U	1	extension tabletop	MDF	19	686	838	
V	2	ext. horizontal supports	hardwood	19	38	610	
W	2	ext. vertical supports	hardwood	19	38	305	
X	1	ext. center supports	hardwood	19	38	267	
Y	1	outfeed tabletop	MDF	19	686	1626	
Z	1	outfeed top front cleat	hardwood	19	32	1626	
AA	2	rear leg vertical supports	hardwood	19	38	711	
BB	2	rear leg horizontal supports	hardwood	19	38	1588	
CC	4	rear leg corner braces	hardwood	19	133	133	angle-cut
DD	2	rear adjustable legs	hardwood	19	38	406	

HARDWARE

8 Locking wheel casters

2 - 559mm Drawer glide sets

Adjustable shelf pins as detailed

2 - 107° Hidden hinges

8 Knobs

8 Hanger bolts, 51mm-long x 6mm-diameter thread

Door and drawer handles as detailed

Electrical switch, plug and junction boxes

Screws as detailed

Glue

51mm PB screws

Biscuits

32mm Screws

Brad nails

16mm Screws

38mm Screws

38mm-Long by 6mm-diameter carriage bolts with washers & nuts

T-square fence system

51mm Wood screws

STEP 1 ■ Cut the top and bottom boards A to the size indicated in the materials list. Each panel requires two ³⁄₄"-wide dadoes and two ³⁄₄"-wide rabbets. All of the cuts are ¹⁄₄" deep. Refer to the illustration for positioning.

STEP 2 ■ The four upright panels B are attached to the top and bottom boards in the dadoes and rabbets. Use glue and four 2" PB screws per end, in pilot holes, to secure the panels.

STEP 3 ■ The back C is attached to the carcass using biscuits and glue. If you don't have a biscuit joiner, screws and glue will work just as well.

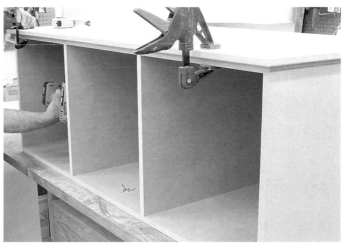

STEP 4 ■ The finished top D is a ³⁄₄"-thick piece of MDF with the upper and lower edges rounded over. Use a ¹⁄₄"-radius roundover bit in your router to ease these edges. The front and both sides overhang the cabinet carcass by 1". Use glue and 1¹⁄₄" screws, from the underside, to attach the top board. Four screws per section will be enough to secure the top.

STEP 5 ■ The left-end compartment will be used as a dust collection chamber. Install the two deflectors E by first cutting the edges at 45° and securing them to the cabinet bottom board and panels using glue and brad nails.

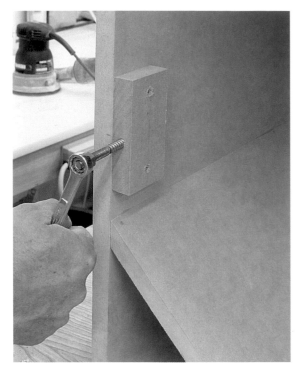

STEP 6 ▪ Two support cleats F are attached to the dust chamber side panels with glue and 1¼" screws. They are aligned flush with the front edges of the vertical panels. Drill pilot holes in the center edge of each cleat to accept the wood screw end of ¼"-diameter hanger bolts. Leave about 1" of the ¼"-diameter machine thread in front of the cleat's edge so a handle can be threaded onto the shaft.

STEP 7 ▪ Cut the dust chamber door panel G to the size indicated in the materials list and round over its front face edge with a ¼"-radius router bit. Hold the door so its bottom edge is flush with the bottom face of the bottom board and press it into the hanger bolts to mark their location. The door overlays each vertical partition by ⅜". Drill ⅜"-diameter holes in the panel and attach it to the cabinet with ¼" threaded knobs on the hanger bolts. The hanger bolts and knobs are available at many woodworking and home improvement stores.

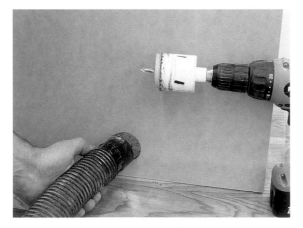

STEP 8 ▪ Drill a hole as low as possible between the dust chamber deflectors through the backboard of the cabinet. This hole will be used to attach a vacuum hose. My vacuum, along with many others on the market, comes with a 2¼"-outside-diameter hose. This is a common hose size, but you should check the size of your hose before drilling the hole. The hole diameter can be as large as 4", with an appropriate fitting, if you plan on using a large dust collection system.

STEP 9 ▪ The center section is 18½" wide and will contain two drawers. My drawer boxes are 17½" wide. They are 22"-deep by 6"-high, made with ¾"-thick MDF.

Cut all the drawer parts H, J and K and assemble by attaching the sides H to the back and front boards J using glue and 2" PB screws. Keep the screws at least 1" away from any edge to avoid splitting the MDF.

Once the sides are secured to the back and front boards, install the bottom using glue and screws. If the bottom board has been cut square, your drawer box will be square.

STEP 10 ▪ Install the drawer glides on the drawer boxes and inside the cabinet. Use ¾- or full-extension glides, installing them following the manufacturer's instructions. One set of glides is mounted at the bottom of the cabinet, and the other set is attached 8" above the bottom board.

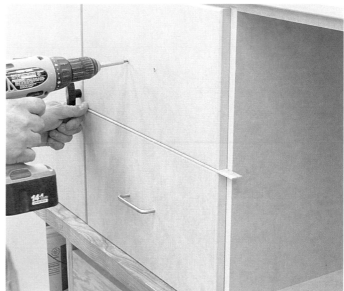

STEP 11 ▪ The drawer faces L are secured to the drawer boxes using 1¼" screws through the back face of each front drawer board. I made the total height of the two drawer faces the same as the dust chamber door. Leave a ⅛" gap between the faces so each one will measure 8³⁄₁₆" high. The drawer faces will overlay each vertical partition edge by ¼" so the faces are 19" wide.

Use a ¼" roundover router bit to ease the front face edges of each door panel, then install the handles of your choice.

STEP 12 ▪ You can add an adjustable shelf to the right-side compartment if required. For drilling the shelf-pin holes, you can make a jig with a 3"-wide by 15½"-high piece of ¾"-thick sheet material scrap. Drill a series of holes in the jig, spacing them about 1¼" apart. Place a short piece of wood dowel on the drill bit, leaving about 1¼" of drill bit exposed. Drill two columns of holes in each vertical partition in that section using the jig and drill stop. You'll get accurately aligned holes without drilling all the way through the cabinet sides.

STEP 13 ▪ Cut the shelf board M to size. Install adjustable shelf pins in the holes and put the shelf in place.

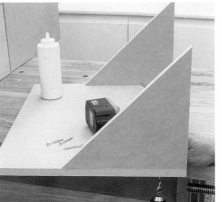

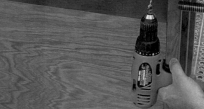

STEP 15 ■ The left side of this saw cabinet has a platform that will hold my vacuum cleaner. Check the dimensions of your vacuum cleaner to verify it will fit before cutting the parts.

I have cut and attached two support boards Q, cut in the shape of a triangle, to help secure the platform. Use glue and 2" screws to attach the angle supports to the stand base.

STEP 14 ■ The right-end cabinet door N is made of ³⁄₄" MDF with the front face edges rounded over using a ¹⁄₄"-radius router bit. It's 16¹⁄₂" high to align with the tops of the drawer faces, and is mounted using 107° full-overlay hidden hinges. Normally, door width is determined by adding 1" to the interior dimension of the cabinet. However, I'm sharing a partition with the drawer faces, so I've added ³⁄₄" to the interior width so my door will be 20" wide. Drill two 35mm holes, 4" from the top and bottom edges, with the holes ¹⁄₈" from the door edge. Install the hinges with mounting plates attached.

Hold the door in the open position, 90° to the face of the cabinet, and put a ¹⁄₈" spacer between the door and cabinet edge. Drive ⁵⁄₈" screws through the plates to secure the hinges to the cabinet sides. Check the door fit and adjust.

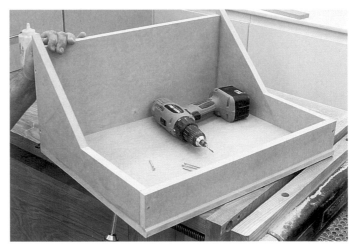

STEP 16 ■ The rails R, S and T are 3" high and attached to the base with screws and glue. The front and back rails are straight, while the side rails are angle-cut on one end at 45° to meet the angle supports.

STEP 17 ■ Attach the vacuum stand to the cabinet carcass, aligning it flush with the underside of the bottom board. Use 1¹⁄₂" screws through the back rail into the cabinet side boards to secure the platform.

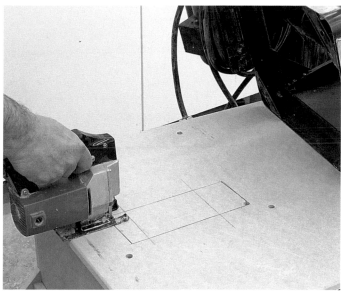

STEP 18 ■ I used 4"-high, heavy-duty locking wheels on my saw station. They are attached with 1½"-long by ¼"-diameter carriage bolts through the cabinet base board. The wheels are located directly under the center panels and as close to the right end as possible. The left-end casters are positioned halfway under the cabinet, and the other half of the caster flange supports the vacuum stand. Push the carriage bolts through the holes in the base board and secure the casters with washers and nuts.

STEP 19 ■ Locate your benchtop saw on top of the cabinet, above the dust chamber where it will be permanently attached. The table saw blade throws most of its dust ahead and directly below the blade. Mark the hold-down bolt locations as well as the leading edge position of the saw blade on the cabinet top. Cut a large hole in the tabletop through the two layers into the dust chamber. Most of the dust will be directed into the hole by the blade, and the vacuum cleaner will draw air through that hole to collect the dust. Test the dust collection and adjust the hole size if necessary.

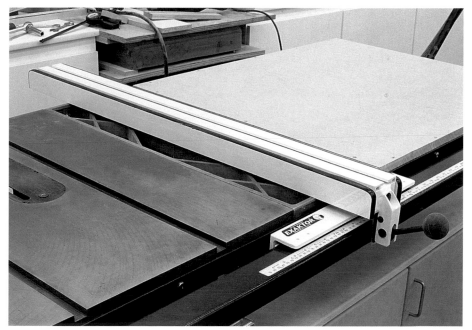

STEP 20 ■ I wired my saw to a switch with a power-indicator light. Your saw may already have a switch, so this step won't be needed. However, if you do need one and are uncomfortable with electrical wiring, call a professional.

I also installed a switched plug to control my vacuum cleaner. Both electrical boxes are surface mounted to the cabinet top in front of the table saw.

STEP 21 ■ The best upgrade for your table saw is a high-quality T-square fence system. Older saws often had poorly designed fences that were sometimes hard to keep in adjustment and required constant maintenance. The new fences are accurate, well built and easy to align. Many of the new T-square fence systems, like this model from Exaktor Woodworking Tools, come with a rear angle bar that provides support for an extended table.

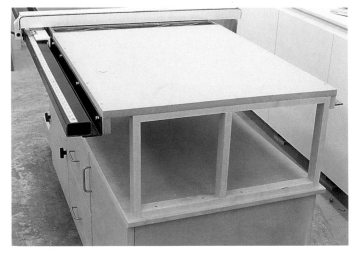

STEP 22 ■ The extension table material is ¾"-thick MDF with a hardwood frame. The length of panel U will depend on the model of T-square fence you purchase and the remaining distance on your cabinet after a table saw has been installed.

STEP 23 ■ The outfeed table is also made with ¾"-thick MDF. The front edge that rests on the table saw support bracket has a hardwood spacer, cleat Z, to level the outfeed tabletop's surface to the bench saw top surface. I will be supporting the front edge of my outfeed table on the angle bar that was supplied with the T-square fence I installed. If you don't have the fence upgrade, attach metal angle stock or a hardwood cleat to the back of your saw.

STEP 24 ■ The rear leg assembly (AA and BB) is made with ¾"-thick by 1½"-wide hardwood. Use 2" wood screws and glue to build the assembly. I wanted to keep the weight to a minimum, so I used this light-duty leg system. Most of the support will be provided at the front edge of this table because it's attached to the saw. When not in use, lower the saw blade and move your fence to the far right end of the saw, then rest the table on top and wheel the workstation to its storage area.

The frame is about three-quarters of the distance between the floor and underside of the outfeed table, or 28" in my case. Attach the leg frame to the underside of the outfeed table with glue and 1¼" screws.

STEP 25 ■ Cut two adjustable legs DD about 16" long and rout a ¼"-wide slot in the center of each one starting and stopping 2" from each end. Use ¼"-diameter hanger bolts and knobs to attach the adjustable legs to the leg frame. Position the hanger bolts so they can be adjusted 2" above and below the correct table height, assuming the workstation is resting on a level floor.

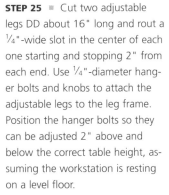

STEP 26 ■ Install two ¼"-diameter hanger bolts into the bottom edge of the front support cleat on the outfeed table. Align the table on the rear support of your saw and drill a ⅜"-diameter hole at each end to match the position of the hanger bolts. Attach the outfeed table to the saw by placing the hanger bolt shafts in the holes and securing them with the proper-size knobs.

STEP 27 ▪ Rout slots in the outfeed table in line with the table saw's miter slide slots.

You will need about four sheets of ¾"-thick MDF and one 10' length of 1x6 hardwood for the cabinet construction, plus the hardware as noted.

I used MDF, but any sheet material is suitable, so pick one that meets your budget and preference. Melamine particleboard would be a good choice or, if you prefer, any plywood with a smooth surface.

This is the perfect saw cabinet if your workshop is located in a garage. At the end of each woodworking session the entire station can be quickly pushed against a wall. The cabinet can be used as a static saw station by replacing the wheels with a simple base frame.

Final table saw height is the most important issue to deal with before starting construction. There are many types of benchtop saws and all of them are different heights and widths. The cabinet tabletop should be suitable for most saws, if not all, but it would be wise to verify the depth of your equipment before cutting the sheet material to size. Wheel assemblies also come in different heights, so purchase the style you want before starting the project.

STEP 28 ▪ If you plan on doing a lot of crosscutting on your saw workstation, consider buying one of the new sliding table systems. They increase the flexibility of the saw and let you cut wide panels easily and with increased safety. Some of the table systems, like this Exaktor EX26 table, have a release feature that will let you quickly install and remove the unit without disturbing any adjustments.

STEP 29 ▪ The extended side table is a great place to install a router. The workstation can then be used for sawing and router work because the T-square fence system is used for both operations.

BUILDING A TABLE SAW CROSSCUTTING SLED

materials list ▪ **INCHES**

QUANTITY	PART	STOCK	THICKNESS	WIDTH	LENGTH	COMMENTS
1	platform	plywood	³/₄	30	36	
2	runners	hardwood	³/₈	³/₄	30	
2	fences	2x4 stock	1¹/₂	3¹/₂	36	
1	blade guard	2x4 stock	1¹/₂	3¹/₂	10	

HARDWARE

1" Screws

Glue

materials list ▪ **MILLIMETERS**

QUANTITY	PART	STOCK	THICKNESS	WIDTH	LENGTH	COMMENTS
1	platform	plywood	19	762	914	
2	runners	hardwood	10	19	762	
2	fences	2x4 stock	38	89	914	
1	blade guard	2x4 stock	38	89	254	

HARDWARE

25mm Screws

Glue

A crosscutting sled is one of the handiest and safest table saw accessories you'll ever own. It is simple to build and a real pleasure to use when cutting wide panels.

STEP 1 ▪ Cut the platform, making sure it's accurately sized and square. Cut the two hardwood runners and test fit them in the table saw miter grooves. A proper fit will allow the runners to run freely with minimal side play. Attach the runners to the platform with 1" screws and glue. Make sure they're accurately spaced to match the table saw grooves.

STEP 2 ▪ Using your saw fence and a framing square, install the back rail with screws and glue and align it at 90° to the fence.

STEP 3 ▪ Install the front rail using the same procedures.

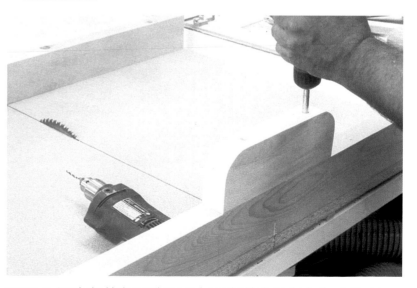

STEP 4 ▪ Attach the blade guard centered over the blade on the back rail. Round over each end of the guard board with a belt sander to eliminate the sharp corners.

Router Table Cabinet

I've seen a lot of router table systems, tried many and had a number of different designs in my shop over the years. However, I always found something lacking in the designs and often promised myself that I would build a router table cabinet to suit my needs one day. Well, that day has arrived, and I'm pleased with the results.

My list of design demands included an adjustable fence that had an opening range of at least 12". How many times have you wanted to run a groove in a wide board and couldn't because your router fence system opened only a couple of inches? My dream table had to have a miter slide track, be at least 35" high and have a large, solid-surface table to support boards properly. I was really tired of balancing large panels on small flimsy tables.

Accessory storage and proper dust collection rounded out my list of "wants" for the ideal router cabinet. I hesitate to say ultimate router station because there's always something miss-

ing that I'll discover later, but this cabinet is close to perfect for my work and it didn't cost a fortune to build.

I used ¾"-thick MDF sheet material. It's a great board for this application because the MDF is heavy, which will keep the cabinet stable, and it's easy to machine. I've detailed two leg options, one for a movable cabinet and the other for a cabinet that will be permanently located. The knobs and aluminum tracks are available at all woodworking outlets and are reasonably priced.

Have fun building of this router cabinet. You'll have easy access to the router and good dust collection. I'm sure you'll appreciate the bit storage slide-outs and great storage drawers for all your router accessories.

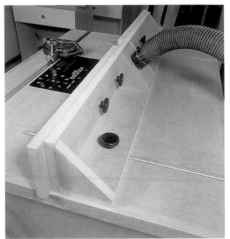

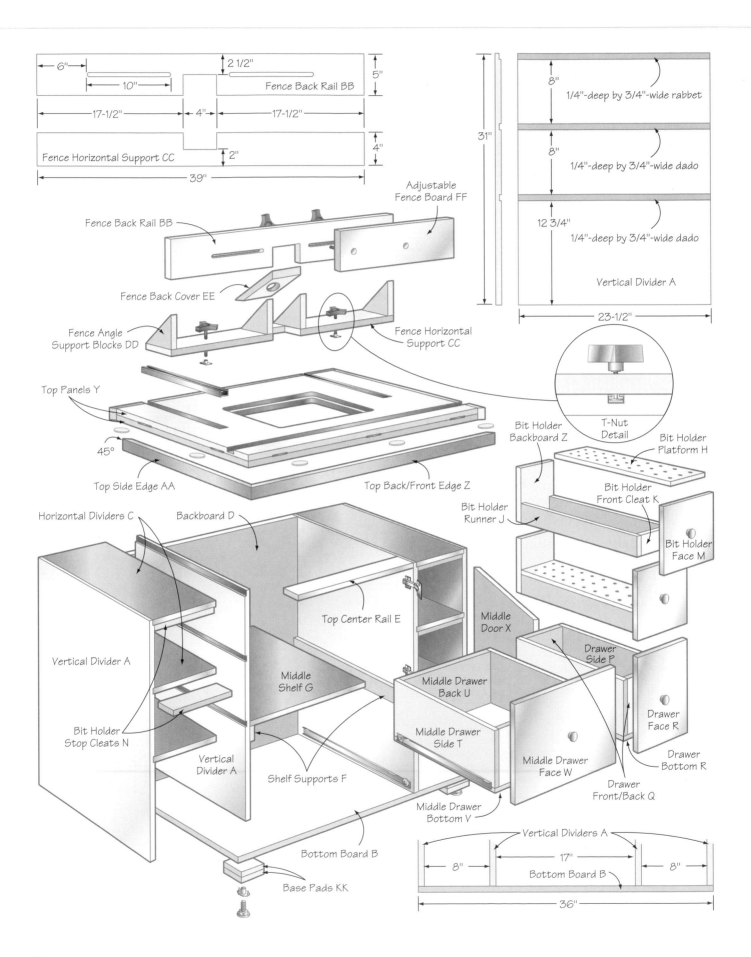

6"

10"

2 1/2"

5"

Fence Back Rail BB

17-1/2"

4"

17-1/2"

Fence Horizontal Support CC

2"

4"

39"

31"

8"

1/4"-deep by 3/4"-wide rabbet

8"

1/4"-deep by 3/4"-wide dado

12 3/4"

1/4"-deep by 3/4"-wide dado

Vertical Divider A

23-1/2"

Fence Back Rail BB

Adjustable
Fence Board FF

Fence Back Cover EE

Fence Angle
Support Blocks DD

Fence Horizontal
Support CC

T-Nut
Detail

Top Panels Y

Bit Holder
Backboard Z

Bit Holder
Platform H

Bit Holder
Front Cleat K

45°

Top Side Edge AA

Top Back/Front Edge Z

Bit Holder
Runner J

Bit Holder
Face M

Horizontal Dividers C

Backboard D

Vertical Divider A

Top Center Rail E

Middle
Door X

Drawer
Side P

Bit Holder
Stop Cleats N

Middle
Shelf G

Middle Drawer
Back U

Drawer
Face R

Vertical
Divider A

Shelf Supports F

Middle Drawer
Side T

Middle Drawer
Face W

Drawer
Bottom R

Bottom Board B

Middle Drawer
Bottom V

Drawer
Front/Back Q

Base Pads KK

Vertical Dividers A

8"

17"

8"

Bottom Board B

36"

materials list ▪ **INCHES**

REFERENCE	QUANTITY	PART	STOCK	THICKNESS	WIDTH	LENGTH	COMMENTS
A	4	vertical dividers	MDF	3/4	23 1/2	31	
B	1	bottom board	MDF	3/4	23 1/2	36	
C	6	horizontal dividers	MDF	3/4	8 1/2	23 1/2	
D	1	backboard	MDF	3/4	31 3/4	36	
E	1	top center rail	MDF	3/4	3	17	
F	2	shelf supports	MDF	3/4	3	23 1/2	
G	1	middle shelf	MDF	3/4	17	23 1/2	
H	4	bit holder platforms	MDF	3/4	7 15/16	22	
J	8	bit holder runners	MDF	3/4	2 1/2	22	
K	4	bit holder front cleats	MDF	3/4	2 1/2	6 7/16	
L	4	bit holder backboards	MDF	3/4	7 15/16	7 15/16	
M	4	bit holder front faces	MDF	3/4	9	8 1/2	
N	4	bit holder stop cleats	MDF	3/4	2	8	
P	4	drawer sides	MDF	3/4	9 1/4	22	
Q	4	drawer fronts & backs	MDF	3/4	9 1/4	5 1/2	
R	2	drawer bottoms	MDF	3/4	7	22	
S	2	drawer faces	MDF	3/4	9	13 7/8	
T	2	middle drawer sides	MDF	3/4	7 3/4	22	
U	2	drawer front & back	MDF	3/4	7 3/4	14 1/2	
V	1	drawer bottom	MDF	3/4	16	22	
W	1	middle drawer face	MDF	3/4	17 3/4	13 7/8	
X	1	middle door	MDF	3/4	17 3/4	17 1/4	
Y	2	top panels	MDF	3/4	37 3/4	27 3/4	
Z	2	top back & front edges	hardwood	3/4	1 1/2	39 1/4	
AA	2	top side edges	hardwood	3/4	1 1/2	29 1/4	
BB	1	fence back rail	MDF	3/4	5	39	
CC	1	fence horizontal support	MDF	3/4	4	39	
DD	4	fence angle support blocks	MDF	3/4	4	4	angle-cut
EE	1	fence back cover	MDF	3/4	4	5 1/4	angle-cut
FF	2	adjustable fence boards	MDF	3/4	5	19 1/2	

BASE OPTION #1

REFERENCE	QUANTITY	PART	STOCK	THICKNESS	WIDTH	LENGTH	COMMENTS
GG	2	sides	MDF	3/4	3	20	
HH	2	front & back boards	MDF	3/4	3	4 1/2	
JJ	1	top	MDF	3/4	6	20	
	2	heavy-duty wheels, 3 3/4" high					

BASE OPTION #2

REFERENCE	QUANTITY	PART	STOCK	THICKNESS	WIDTH	LENGTH	COMMENTS
KK	8	base pads	MDF	3/4	3	3	
	4	metal adjustable leveling feet					

HARDWARE

4 Drawer knobs or pulls
3 Sets of 22" drawer glides
2 - 107° Hidden hinges and plates
1 - 48"-Long aluminum miter slide track
1 - 48"-Long aluminum T-track
6 - 1" by 1/4"-Diameter threaded knobs
1 Power bar with switch
11/2" PB screws as detailed
5/8" PB screws as detailed
Glue
Pocket screws
Brad nails
2" Screws
T-nuts

materials list ▪ **MILLIMETERS**

REFERENCE	QUANTITY	PART	STOCK	THICKNESS	WIDTH	LENGTH	COMMENTS
A	4	vertical dividers	MDF	19	597	787	
B	1	bottom board	MDF	19	597	914	
C	6	horizontal dividers	MDF	19	216	597	
D	1	backboard	MDF	19	806	914	
E	1	top center rail	MDF	19	76	432	
F	2	shelf supports	MDF	19	76	597	
G	1	middle shelf	MDF	19	432	597	
H	4	bit holder platforms	MDF	19	202	559	
J	8	bit holder runners	MDF	19	64	559	
K	4	bit holder front cleats	MDF	19	64	163	
L	4	bit holder backboards	MDF	19	202	202	
M	4	bit holder front faces	MDF	19	229	216	
N	4	bit holder stop cleats	MDF	19	51	203	
P	4	drawer sides	MDF	19	235	559	
Q	4	drawer fronts & backs	MDF	19	235	140	
R	2	drawer bottoms	MDF	19	178	559	
S	2	drawer faces	MDF	19	229	352	
T	2	middle drawer sides	MDF	19	197	559	
U	2	drawer front & back	MDF	19	197	369	
V	1	drawer bottom	MDF	19	406	559	
W	1	middle drawer face	MDF	19	451	352	
X	1	middle door	MDF	19	451	438	
Y	2	top panels	MDF	19	959	705	
Z	2	top back & front edges	hardwood	19	38	997	
AA	2	top side edges	hardwood	19	38	743	
BB	1	fence back rail	MDF	19	127	991	
CC	1	fence horizontal support	MDF	19	102	991	
DD	4	fence angle support blocks	MDF	19	102	102	angle-cut
EE	1	fence back cover	MDF	19	102	133	angle-cut
FF	2	adjustable fence boards	MDF	19	127	496	

BASE OPTION #1

REFERENCE	QUANTITY	PART	STOCK	THICKNESS	WIDTH	LENGTH	COMMENTS
GG	2	sides	MDF	19	76	508	
HH	2	front & back boards	MDF	19	76	115	
JJ	1	top	MDF	19	152	508	
	2	heavy-duty wheels, 95mm high					

BASE OPTION #2

REFERENCE	QUANTITY	PART	STOCK	THICKNESS	WIDTH	LENGTH	COMMENTS
KK	8	base pads	MDF	19	76	76	
	4	metal adjustable leveling feet					

HARDWARE

4 Drawer knobs or pulls

3 Sets of 559mm drawer glides

2 - 107° Hidden hinges and plates

1 - 1219mm-Long aluminum miter slide track

1 - 1219mm-Long aluminum T-track

6 - 25mm by 6mm-Diameter threaded knobs

1 Power bar with switch

38mm PB screws as detailed

16mm PB screws as detailed

Glue

Pocket screws

Brad nails

51mm Screws

T-nuts

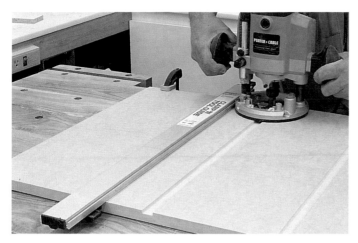

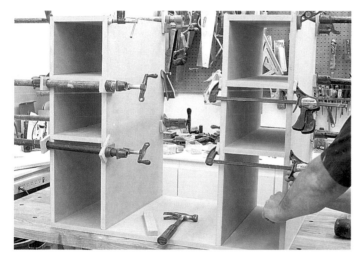

STEP 1 ■ Prepare the four vertical dividers A by cutting them to size and forming the dadoes and rabbets in each panel as shown. All the rabbets and dadoes are ¾" wide by ¼" deep.

STEP 2 ■ The bottom board B is secured to the dividers with glue and 1½" screws in pilot holes. Align the two sets of dividers, spaced 8" apart, with the dadoes and rabbets facing each other. The middle section should be 17" wide between panels. Keep the screws 1" away from any panel end and use four screws per divider, driven through the bottom board.

STEP 3 ■ Install the six horizontal dividers C in the dadoes and rabbets. Use glue and clamps to secure the sections.

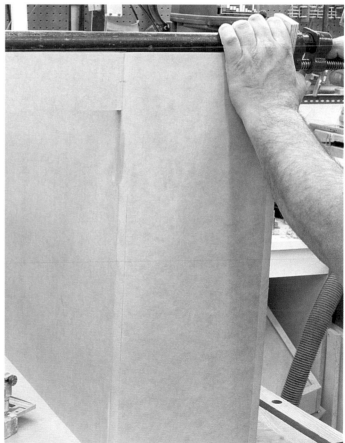

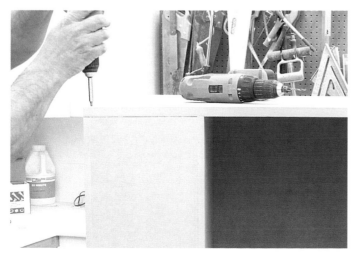

STEP 4 ■ Attach the backboard D to the cabinet using glue and 1½" screws. If you've carefully cut the back panel square, the cabinet will be properly aligned.

STEP 5 ■ The top center rail E is attached with one ¾"-thick edge facing forward. Secure it with biscuits, or pocket screws and glue if you don't have a biscuit joiner. This rail will be attached to the underside of the tabletop.

This cabinet is on its back with the top facing the camera.

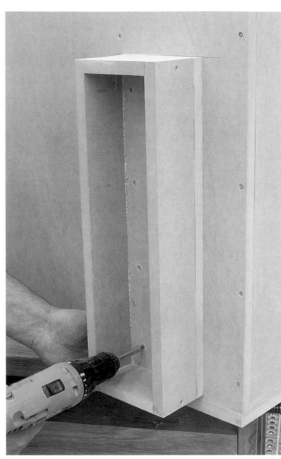

STEP 7 ■ The other half of base option #1 is a box made with ¾" MDF using the parts GG, HH and JJ. It's attached to the bottom of the cabinet with 1¼" screws and glue. If the cabinet has to be moved often, you can lift the fixed base end and push it along the floor on the wheels.

The height of my fixed base portion is 3¾" to match the wheel height. If you do use this setup, purchase the wheels first so the correct height can be verified. After installing both options, I've decided to use base #2 on my cabinet, as described in step 29.

STEP 6 ■ If you plan to use base option #1, attach two heavy-duty locking wheel assemblies to one side of the cabinet.

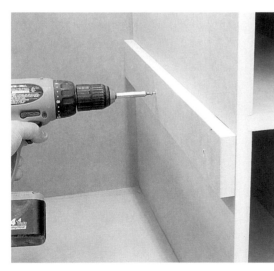

STEP 8 ■ Install the two shelf supports F in the middle section. They are secured with glue and 1¼" screws. Their top edges are 12¾" above the bottom board. Cut the middle shelf G to the size indicated in the materials list and secure it to the cleats with glue and brad nails.

STEP 9 ■ The four bit holder slide-outs are made with ¾"-thick MDF. Each holder board has a series of holes for ¼"- and ½"-diameter router bits. I spaced my holes 2" apart with the two outside rows 1½" in from each board's edge and the third row in the center.

The holder platforms H are attached to the runners J with glue and 1½" screws. The runners are flush with the outside long edges of the holder platforms. A front lower cleat K is also attached to the holder platform in the same way. The backboards L are attached to the rear of each assembly with glue and 1½" screws. Use a ¼" roundover bit in your router to soften the front edges of the slide-out faces M. Once the face is aligned on the slide-out, attach each face with 1¼" screws through the front lower cleat.

STEP 10 ■ Cut and attach the four stop cleats N with glue and 1¼"-long screws. These cleats will stop the slide-out when fully extended. When it's necessary to remove or install the slide-outs, simply tip them upward to move past the stop cleats.

STEP 11 ■ The two outside lower drawer boxes are 7" wide by 10" high by 22" deep and made with ¾"-thick MDF. Attach the drawer sides P to the back and front boards Q using glue and 1½" screws. The bottom boards R are also secured to the sides, front and bottom board edges with 1½" screws and glue to form the drawer boxes. Use 22" bottom-mount drawer glides, or full-extension glides if you prefer, to install the drawer boxes in the cabinet.

STEP 12 ■ The lower outside drawer box faces S have their front edges rounded over using a ¼" router bit. They are secured to the drawer boxes with 1¼" screws through the inside of the box. Install the faces so they are aligned with the slide-out fronts, leaving a ⅛" gap between each front.

STEP 13 ■ The lower middle drawer box is 8½" high by 16" wide by 22" deep. Build the box using ¾" MDF with parts T, U and V following the same steps as the outside lower drawer boxes. Mount this box using 22" drawer glides.

STEP 14 ■ Round over the front edges of drawer face W using a ¼" router bit. Attach it to the drawer box with 1¼" screws, being careful to leave equal spacing on both sides, with its top aligned to the two outside drawer faces.

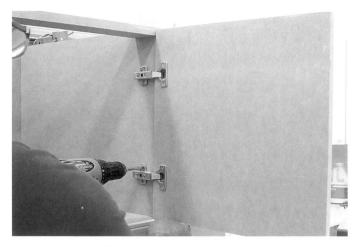

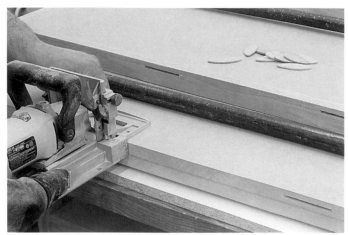

STEP 15 ■ Cut the door X to size and round over the front face edges. I used full-overlay 107° hinges with standard mounting plates. Drill 35mm holes, $\frac{1}{8}$" from the door edge, to secure the hinges. Hold the door in its normally open position, with a $\frac{1}{8}$"-thick spacer between the door and cabinet edge, and secure the mounting plates with $\frac{5}{8}$" screws.

STEP 16 ■ The top is made by gluing two $\frac{3}{4}$"-thick MDF panels together. Cut both panels Y a little oversize so they can be trimmed to a finished size when the adhesive has cured. The top is banded with $1\frac{1}{2}$"-high by $\frac{3}{4}$"-thick hardwood and is secured in place with biscuits. Cut the edges Z and AA to size with 45° miters on each end to join the corners.

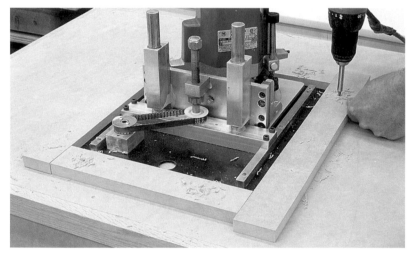

STEP 17 ■ Turn the top upside down on the router cabinet. It should overhang the front edge by $1\frac{1}{2}$" and the sides by $1\frac{5}{8}$". I will be using a Rout-R-Lift plate made by JessEm Tool Company, but any plate can be installed using the following method. Place the router plate on the center of the table and 5" back from the front edge of the top. Fasten strips of wood around the plate with screws. These strips will be used as a template to guide your router.

STEP 18 ■ The router base should have a bushing guide installed to run against the strips of wood. The size of the bushing should equal the depth of cut for the wing or slot cutter bit that will be used to form a groove on the top side of the table to inset the router plate flush with the top face. My wing bit cuts $\frac{1}{2}$" deep, so I want the hole to be smaller than the strip edges by $\frac{1}{2}$" on all sides. Cut the hole using the guide bushing and router bit.

STEP 19 ■ Flip the top right side up and use the wing cutter to groove the top. The router plate should be flush with the tabletop's surface. I hand-formed the corners to match my router plate. It may also be necessary in your case to use a sharp knife and chisel to carve the corners. Fasten the top to the cabinet using 2" screws through the horizontal supports and middle top rail.

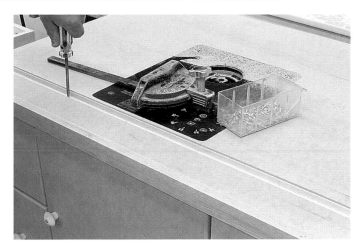

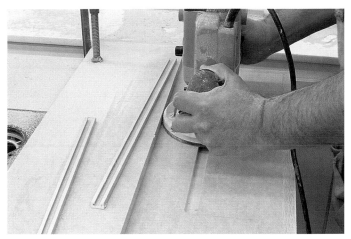

STEP 20 ▪ I installed a ³⁄₄" miter slide track in my tabletop. Cut the groove for the slide track as close to the front edge of your router plate as possible. This track required a 1"-wide groove cut parallel to the router plate. I drilled the track and secured it to the top with ⁵⁄₈" screws. The track is available through most woodworking supply stores.

STEP 21 ▪ The T-track, which will be used to lock the adjustable fence, is also attached to the top in grooves. Rout the grooves on each side, parallel to the plate, and match the size of track you purchased, making sure they are flush with the tabletop surface. Once again, the tracks are secured with ⁵⁄₈" screws.

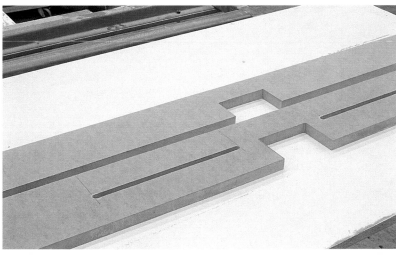

STEP 22 ▪ All of the fence parts are made with ³⁄₄"-thick MDF. The fence back rail BB has two ³⁄₈"-wide grooves routed into the center and through the board. The grooves start 6" from each end and stop 16" from each end. This rail also requires a 4"-wide by 2¹⁄₂"-high notch, centered on the length of the board. The horizontal support CC also has a notch that is 4" wide by 2" high in the center of the board. Both notches can be cut with a band saw or jigsaw.

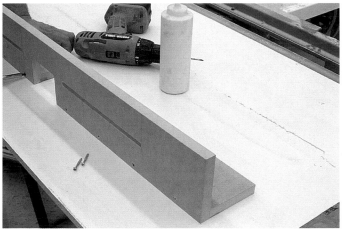

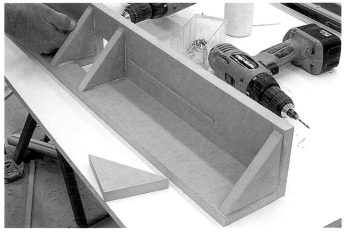

STEP 23 ▪ Attach the fence back rail BB to the horizontal support CC with 1¹⁄₂" screws and glue at about 4" on center.

STEP 24 ▪ The four right-angle fence supports DD are 4" x 4" blocks of ³⁄₄" MDF cut at 45°. Use glue and 1¹⁄₂" screws to attach the supports to the fence assembly. One support is installed at either end and the remaining two on each side of the cutout notch in the fence boards.

STEP 25 ■ The back cover EE for the fence cutout has a 45° miter on both ends. Apply glue to all edges and secure the cover with a few brad nails on the top and bottom edge.

STEP 26 ■ Drill a 2¼"-diameter hole in the center of the back cover. This will be used to friction-fit a vacuum hose.

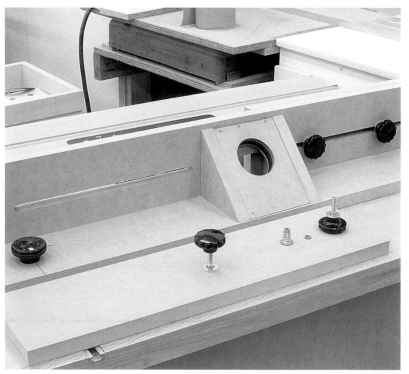

STEP 27 ■ Center the fence assembly on the router table and drill two ⅜"-diameter holes in the horizontal support over the center of each T-track. Use a T-nut and knob with a 1"-long by ¼"-diameter threaded shaft screwed into the nut. Tighten the knobs and verify that the fence locks securely.

STEP 28 ■ The adjustable fence boards FF have two T-nuts driven into the front faces. Counterbore the hole so the nuts are slightly below the fence face. Position the nuts so both fences can come together in the center and travel about 4" out from the center.

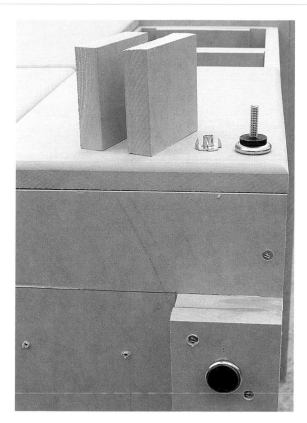

STEP 29 ▪ I will be using base option #2, as illustrated. Two pads KK are glued together and attached to the bottom, 3" back from the front edge of the cabinet and on both back corners. Drill holes for $\frac{1}{4}$"-diameter T-nuts and install a threaded metal foot in the center of each block as shown.

You will need four sheets of $\frac{3}{4}$"-thick MDF to build this cabinet. I used about 13' of hardwood to edge the top, as well.

I used MDF, but any $\frac{3}{4}$" sheet material will be fine, and the same construction dimensions and procedures can be used. If you decide to use another material, look for a smooth surface so your router work will slide easily on the top.

Pay special attention to the final height of your cabinet. My cabinet, with the adjustable legs in base option #2, puts my top surface at about 35" above the floor. That's a comfortable height for me, but your requirements may be different. Adjust the vertical divider heights to meet your needs.

All of the aluminum track, knobs and related hardware are sold at most woodworking stores. Woodworkers tend to make jigs and shop-built tool accessories, so this line of hardware has become very popular.

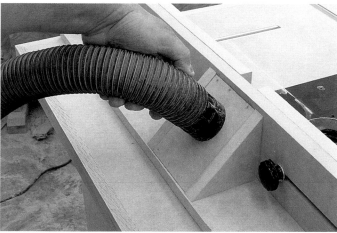

STEP 30 ▪ My $2\frac{1}{4}$"-outside-diameter vacuum hose on my shop vacuum is a snug fit in the dust hole and provides good particle removal.

I considered adding a dust collection port in the router compartment, but the dust doesn't seem to be that great a problem. My vacuum pulls most of the dust at the fence; however, routing a material that creates fine dust may cause a buildup in the compartment. If that's the case, drilling a dust port and making a Y-fitting so the vacuum could collect from the fence and router compartment would be an easy fix.

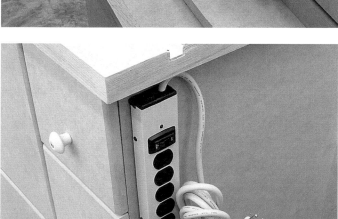

STEP 31 ▪ I purchased and attached a construction-grade power bar, made by Belkin Components, called a Surge-Master HD. This device is designed to control electrical equipment such as saws, compressors and routers. The vacuum cleaner and router will be plugged into the power bar and controlled by a switch. I will also have spare plugs that are overload protected, which I can use in the shop for other electrical equipment.

Drill Press Center

A drill press is a valuable asset in any woodworking shop. Drill presses are available as floor or bench models and have adjustable tables or heads. However, they all lack storage space and have tables that are difficult to adjust.

I built the storage cabinet portion of this project to be used with both floor and bench drill presses. The bench model can be bolted to the top, or the cabinet can be wheeled over the base on floor-model units. If you do own a floor-model press, measure the width and height of the base to be sure the cabinet can be rolled over the base. If the base is too large, change the cabinet dimensions to suit your drill press.

The full-extension top cabinet drawer can hold drill bits on an indexed board, while the remaining drawers can contain accessories, literature and other tools used with your drill press. If you need the drill press table on your floor-model unit lower than the cabinet height, simply roll it out of the way.

Bench-model presses can be mounted on the top, and the station, both cabinet and drill press, can be rolled to any area of your shop.

Many woodworkers will appreciate the wide adjustable table. It can be tipped for angular drilling to the front or rear of your drill press. The adjustable fence is an important option that is missing on most drill units. Wood-workers use drill press fences a great deal and often have to clamp a straight-edged board to the press table. This fence is adjustable, easily locked in place and quick to move where needed.

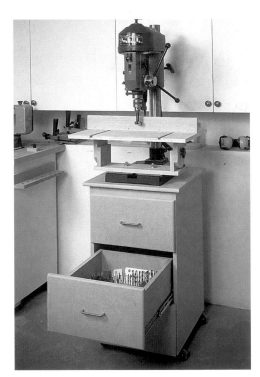

The drill press center is easy to build, inexpensive and well worth the time invested. It's a great workstation to use, and I'm sure you'll quickly appreciate its value.

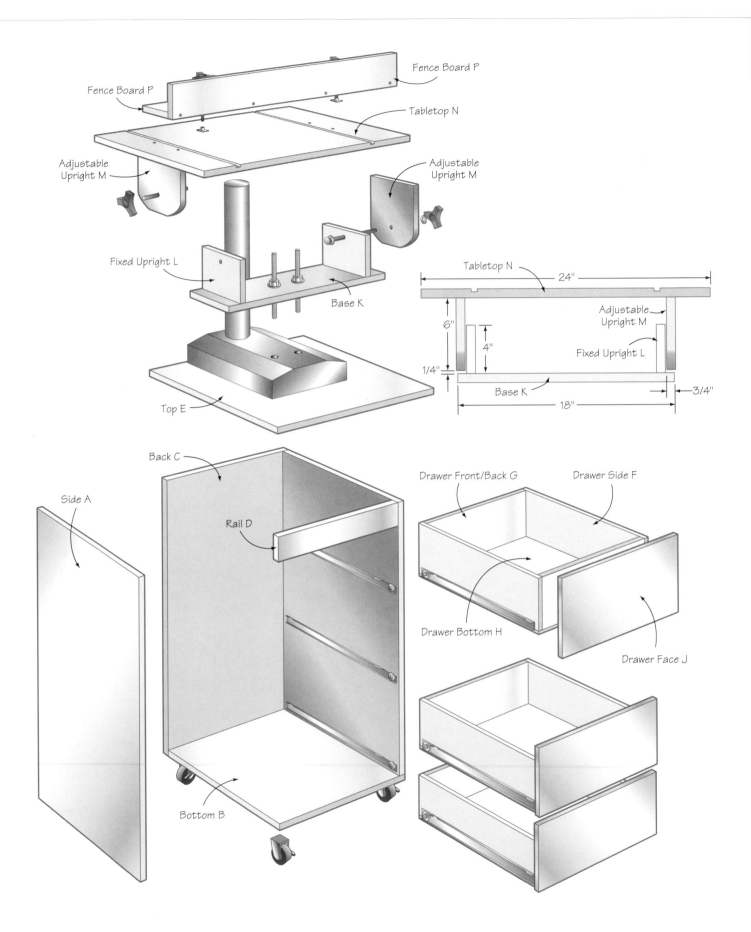

Fence Board P

Fence Board P

Tabletop N

Adjustable
Upright M

Adjustable
Upright M

Fixed Upright L

Base K

Tabletop N

24"

Adjustable
Upright M

6"

4"

Fixed Upright L

1/4"

Base K

3/4"

18"

Top E

Back C

Side A

Drawer Front/Back G

Drawer Side F

Rail D

Drawer Bottom H

Drawer Face J

Bottom B

materials list ■ **INCHES**

REFERENCE	QUANTITY	PART	STOCK	THICKNESS	WIDTH	LENGTH	COMMENTS
CABINET							
A	2	sides	MDF	$3/4$	19	30	
B	1	bottom	MDF	$3/4$	18	19	
C	1	back	MDF	$3/4$	18	$30^3/4$	
D	1	rail	MDF	$3/4$	2	$16^3/4$	
E	1	top	MDF	$3/4$	20	21	
F	6	drawer sides	MDF	$3/4$	$6^1/4$	18	
G	6	drawer fronts & backs	MDF	$3/4$	$6^1/4$	14	
H	3	drawer bottoms	MDF	$3/4$	$15^1/2$	18	
J	3	drawer faces	MDF	$3/4$	$9^5/8$	$17^1/2$	
ADJUSTABLE DRILL TABLE							
K	1	base	hardwood	$3/4$	$5^1/4$	18	
L	2	fixed uprights	hardwood	$3/4$	$5^1/4$	4	
M	2	adjustable uprights	hardwood	$3/4$	$5^1/4$	6	
N	1	tabletop	veneer ply	$3/4$	16	24	
P	2	fence boards	veneer ply	$3/4$	3	24	
Q	2	drill platforms	MDF	$3/4$	14	$16^3/4$	

HARDWARE

Screws as detailed

Glue

3 Drawer handles

3 Sets of full-extension drawer glides

Right-angle brackets

Bolts and nuts as detailed

T-track

T-nuts

Knobs

$1^1/2$" Screws

$5/8$" Screws

$1^1/4$" Screws

4 Wheels

2" Screws

$1/4$" Carriage bolts with washer and knobs

$1/2$" Screws

$1/4$" x 20 Bolt and knob assembly with 1"-long shaft

materials list ■ **MILLIMETERS**

REFERENCE	QUANTITY	PART	STOCK	THICKNESS	WIDTH	LENGTH	COMMENTS
CABINET							
A	2	sides	MDF	19	483	762	
B	1	bottom	MDF	19	457	483	
C	1	back	MDF	19	457	781	
D	1	rail	MDF	19	51	425	
E	1	top	MDF	19	508	533	
F	6	drawer sides	MDF	19	158	457	
G	6	drawer fronts & backs	MDF	19	158	356	
H	3	drawer bottoms	MDF	19	394	457	
J	3	drawer faces	MDF	19	245	445	
ADJUSTABLE DRILL TABLE							
K	1	base	hardwood	19	133	457	
L	2	fixed uprights	hardwood	19	133	102	
M	2	adjustable uprights	hardwood	19	133	152	
N	1	tabletop	veneer ply	19	406	610	
P	2	fence boards	veneer ply	19	76	610	
Q	2	drill platforms	MDF	19	356	425	

HARDWARE

Screws as detailed

Glue

3 Drawer handles

3 Sets of full-extension drawer glides

Right-angle brackets

Bolts and nuts as detailed

T-track

T-nuts

Knobs

38mm Screws

16mm Screws

32mm Screws

4 Wheels

51mm Screws

6mm Carriage bolts with washer and knobs

13mm Screws

6mm x 20 Bolt and knob assembly with 25mm-long shaft

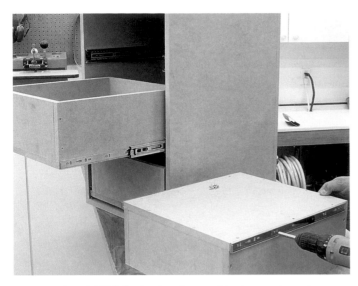

STEP 7 ■ I used 18" full-extension drawer glides to mount my drawer boxes. The bottom drawer is installed as close to the bottom board as possible. The remaining two drawer boxes are installed leaving a 2" space between them.

STEP 8 ■ The drawer faces J are $9\frac{5}{8}$" high by $17\frac{1}{2}$" wide using $\frac{3}{4}$" MDF. The front edges are rounded over with a $\frac{3}{8}$" bit in a router. The bottom drawer face is aligned flush with the bottom edge of the cabinet base board and spaced $\frac{1}{8}$" apart. Secure the faces to the drawer boxes using $1\frac{1}{4}$" screws from inside the drawer box. Attach handles or knobs of your choice.

STEP 9 ■ Install four wheels on the base, setting back the front set by 2". Use medium- or heavy-duty wheels, making sure they are high enough to straddle the drill press base if you own a floor model.

STEP 10 ■ If you are using a benchtop drill press, mount it securely to the cabinet top with bolts or screws. If you own a floor-model press, you can skip this step.

STEP 11 ■ Using hardwood, cut the table base K and the two fixed uprights L to size. Secure both uprights to the base K with glue and 2" screws. The uprights are attached ¾" in from each end of the base K.

STEP 12 ■ Prepare the two adjustable uprights M by cutting them to the size indicated. Remove both lower corners on each board with a 45° cut that's 1½" from each end. Round over the corners with a belt sander, creating an arc on the bottom edge of each upright.

STEP 13 ■ Following the rough shaping with the belt sander, clamp the two uprights together and finish-sand so both have the same profile.

STEP 14 ■ Place the adjustable uprights M on the outside faces of each fixed upright L, aligning the edges of all boards. Use a ¼"-thick spacer under the adjustable uprights and drill a ¼"-diameter hole 3" down from their top edges through both boards. Center the hole on the width of each board and insert a ¼"-diameter carriage bolt, a large washer on the outside face and a knob to lock the uprights together.

STEP 16 ■ The tabletop N is a piece of ¾"-thick veneer plywood. Form two dadoes along the width of the board, 5" in from each edge. The T-track I'm using requires ⅜"-deep dadoes, but your hardware may be different, so verify the track depth before cutting the dadoes. Cut the tracks to length and secure them in the dadoes using ½" screws in countersunk holes at the bottom of the tracks.

STEP 15 ■ Bolt the assembly to the table on your drill press. Each model will have different bolt hole patterns, so choose a method that suits your drill press table. Align the drill chuck center to the center of the table base board and tighten securely.

STEP 17 ■ Attach the top to the adjustable uprights using two 2" screws per upright. Align the top so it's equally spaced on both upright edges, side to side and back to front. Don't use glue in case the top has to be replaced in the future.

STEP 18 ■ The fence is made with $\frac{3}{4}$"-thick veneer plywood. The horizontal and vertical members P are 3" high by 24" long. Attach the vertical board to the horizontal member with glue and four 2" screws. This simple but strong fence can be easily replaced if necessary.

STEP 19 ■ Drill two $\frac{1}{4}$"-diameter holes in the horizontal fence board over the center of each T-track slot. To lock the fence, use a $\frac{1}{4}$" x 20 bolt and knob assembly with a 1"-long shaft screwed to T-nuts in the track.

If you build the drill press center as detailed, you'll need about $1\frac{1}{4}$ sheets of MDF, a 2' x 2' piece of veneer-covered plywood and a 40"-long piece of 1x6 hardwood. The hardware is available at most woodworking stores.

Many configurations are possible for the cabinet, and the final dimensions will depend on the size of your drill press. The sizes shown in this project should be suitable for the majority of floor and benchtop drill presses.

Any $\frac{3}{4}$" sheet material can be used. I decided to use MDF because it's inexpensive, can be easily worked with standard woodworking tools, doesn't require edge finishing and is a stable material. However, particleboard or plywood can be substituted if one of them is a personal favorite of yours.

An additional knob and bolt can be added to double-lock each set of uprights. If you do a lot of heavy work on the drill press, you might want some added insurance that the table will remain level, so add another $\frac{1}{4}$" x 20 bolt and knob to each side. Remove the extra lock when adjustments to the table are needed. However, the one-knob-per-side setup securely locks the table, and it would take quite a bit of weight to move it.

You may want to drill a large round hole in the table to insert a sanding drum. The drum can be installed in the drill chuck and lowered through the hole. The large table and a drum will make a great power sanding accessory on your press. Dozens of drill press accessories are available, such as planers, plug cutters, hollow chisel mortise attachments and so on. The cabinet can be made with one drawer over a door with adjustable shelves or, as shown, three drawers on full-extension (FX) glides. The FX glides are the most expensive part of the project. To reduce costs, use an FX glide set on the drill bit drawer and bottom-mount glides on the remaining drawers.

STEP 20 ■ I'm using one of the drawers, on full-extension drawer glides, to store and index my drill bits. Cut a piece of $\frac{3}{4}$" MDF to size for a drill platform Q. Drill the appropriate holes to store your bits and loosely sit the platform in the drawer box. New holes can be drilled as your bit inventory increases.

Tool Sharpening and Maintenance Station

Sharpening equipment is a necessity in every woodworking shop. Dull tools are aggravating to work with and dangerous. Keeping chisels, turning tools, plane blades and carving tools in good condition is a fact of life in the woodshop.

Many woodworkers use water stones and waterwheel grinders. The stones have to be kept wet to work effectively, so that means a water bath. However, woodworking tools create dust, and when mixed with water, a brown sludge forms in the water bath. Those of you who use oil stones have the same problem with dust — a brown paste covering the stones and lapping plates. I'm sure I've spent more time cleaning the stones and water baths than on actual tool maintenance.

I decided to build a dedicated sharpening station for my 1" belt sander, wet and dry wheel grinder and water bath for my stones. But I vowed to solve the dust and water problems with this station. The flip-up cover is my answer for a dust-free center, and it works great!

This project may not look sleek and stylish, but it keeps my water baths and stones "paste free" and saves me a great deal of time previously wasted cleaning the equipment.

The power cords are routed through the top and plug into a power bar. Two large drawers provide all the space I need for sharpening accessories, extra blades for my tools and manuals related to my equipment. The section below the drawers is enclosed with doors for added dust-free storage. The station is mounted on locking wheels that allow me to bring it to any area in my shop.

If you want clean, almost dust-free sharpening equipment that's ready to use, then this project is for you. The cabinet won't win any beauty awards, but it's number one in the functional category.

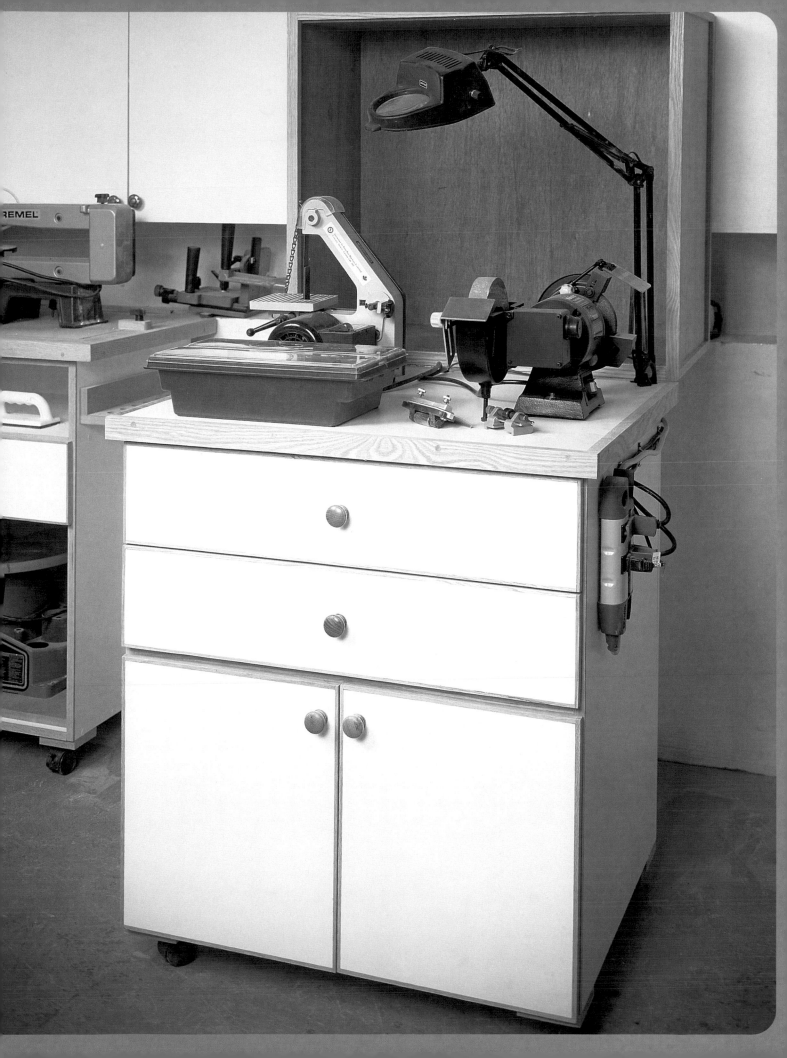

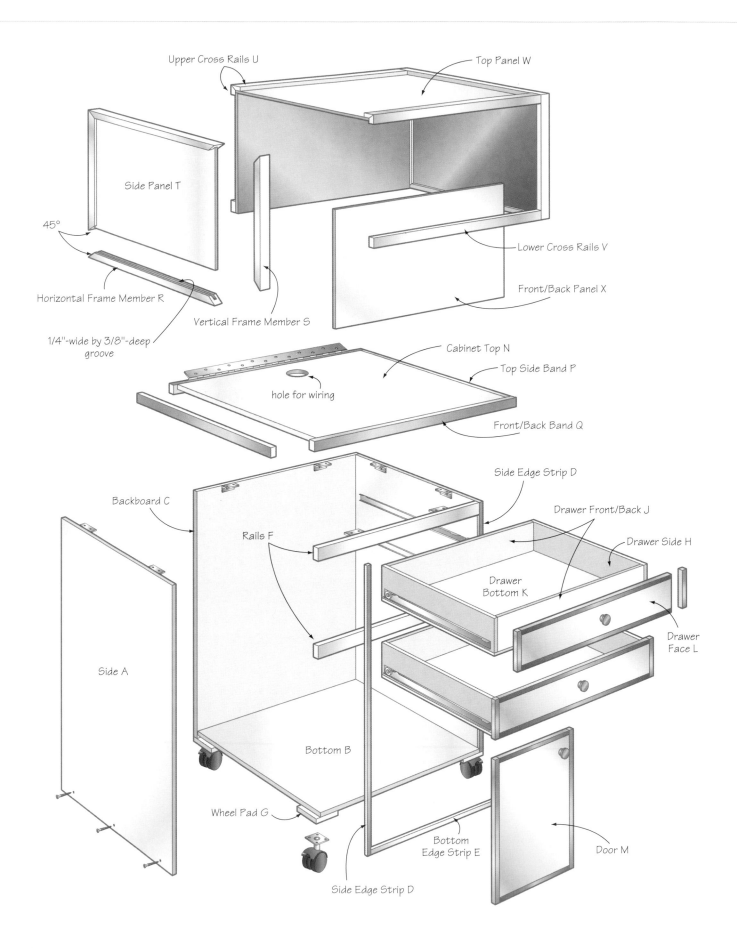

Upper Cross Rails U

Top Panel W

Side Panel T

45°

Horizontal Frame Member R

1/4"-wide by 3/8"-deep groove

Vertical Frame Member S

Lower Cross Rails V

Front/Back Panel X

Cabinet Top N

Top Side Band P

hole for wiring

Front/Back Band Q

Side Edge Strip D

Backboard C

Drawer Front/Back J

Drawer Side H

Rails F

Side A

Drawer Bottom K

Drawer Face L

Bottom B

Door M

Wheel Pad G

Bottom Edge Strip E

Side Edge Strip D

CABINET

REFERENCE	QUANTITY	PART	STOCK	THICKNESS	WIDTH	LENGTH	COMMENTS
A	2	sides	melamine PB	5/8	23³/8	32	
B	1	bottom	melamine PB	5/8	23³/8	28³/4	
C	1	backboard	melamine PB	5/8	30	32	
D	2	side edge strips	hardwood	1/4	5/8	32	
E	1	bottom edge strip	hardwood	1/4	5/8	28³/4	
F	2	rails	hardwood	3/4	1¹/2	28³/4	
G	4	wheel pads	hardwood	3/4	3¹/2	3¹/2	
H	4	drawer sides	melamine PB	5/8	4³/8	22	
J	4	drawer fronts & backs	melamine PB	5/8	4³/8	26¹/2	
K	2	drawer bottoms	melamine PB	5/8	22	27³/4	
L	2	drawer faces	melamine PB	5/8	6¹/2	29³/4	
M	2	doors	melamine PB	5/8	14⁷/8	17¹/2	
N	1	cabinet top	melamine PB	5/8	30¹/4	26¹/2	
P	2	top side bands	hardwood	3/4	1¹/2	26¹/2	
Q	2	front & back bands	hardwood	3/4	1¹/2	31³/4	

COVER

REFERENCE	QUANTITY	PART	STOCK	THICKNESS	WIDTH	LENGTH	COMMENTS
R	4	horizontal frame members	hardwood	3/4	1	28	angle-cut
S	4	vertical frame members	hardwood	3/4	1	16	angle-cut
T	2	side panels	veneer ply	1/4	15¹/4	27¹/4	
U	4	upper cross rails	hardwood	3/4	1¹/2	29³/4	angle-cut
V	2	lower cross rails	hardwood	3/4	1¹/2	29³/4	
W	1	top panel	veneer ply	1/4	30³/8	26³/8	
X	2	front & back panels	veneer ply	1/4	30³/8	14¹/4	

HARDWARE

8 Metal right-angle brackets

2" PB screws as detailed

Brad nails as detailed

Glue

White screw head cover caps as detailed

4 Locking wheels

Iron-on edge tape

2 – 22" Drawer glide sets

4 Knobs

4 – 107° Hidden hinges

1 – 28" Piano hinge

12" Length of small chain

1 Handle

1 Wire grommet

Metal angle brackets

Pocket screws

1¹/4" Screws

5/8" Screws

1" Screws

¹/2" Screws

Biscuits

Wood plugs

Wire protector

materials list ■ **MILLIMETERS**

REFERENCE	QUANTITY	PART	STOCK	THICKNESS	WIDTH	LENGTH	COMMENTS
CABINET							
A	2	sides	melamine PB	16	594	813	
B	1	bottom	melamine PB	16	594	730	
C	1	backboard	melamine PB	16	762	813	
D	2	side edge strips	hardwood	6	16	813	
E	1	bottom edge strip	hardwood	6	16	730	
F	2	rails	hardwood	19	38	730	
G	4	wheel pads	hardwood	19	89	89	
H	4	drawer sides	melamine PB	16	112	559	
J	4	drawer fronts & backs	melamine PB	16	112	673	
K	2	drawer bottoms	melamine PB	16	559	705	
L	2	drawer faces	melamine PB	16	165	756	
M	2	doors	melamine PB	16	378	445	
N	1	cabinet top	melamine PB	16	768	673	
P	2	top side bands	hardwood	19	38	673	
Q	2	front & back bands	hardwood	19	38	806	
COVER							
R	4	horizontal frame members	hardwood	19	25	711	angle-cut
S	4	vertical frame members	hardwood	19	25	406	angle-cut
T	2	side panels	veneer ply	6	387	692	
U	4	upper cross rails	hardwood	19	38	756	angle-cut
V	2	lower cross rails	hardwood	19	38	756	
W	1	top panel	veneer ply	6	772	670	
X	2	front & back panels	veneer ply	6	772	362	

HARDWARE

8 Metal right-angle brackets

51mm PB screws as detailed

Brad nails as detailed

Glue

White screw head cover caps as detailed

4 Locking wheels

Iron-on edge tape

2 – 559mm Drawer glide sets

4 Knobs

4 – 107° Hidden hinges

1 – 711mm Piano hinge

305mm Length of small chain

1 Handle

1 Wire grommet

Metal angle brackets

Pocket screws

32mm Screws

16mm Screws

25mm Screws

6mm Screws

Biscuits

Wood plugs

Wire protector

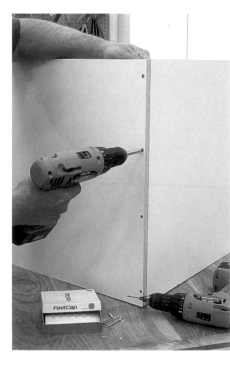

STEP 1 ■ Join the sides A to the bottom board B by drilling 2" PB screws in pilot holes. Cover the screw heads with white stick-on caps or plastic covers.

STEP 2 ■ Apply iron-on edge tape to both long vertical edges of backboard C. Attach the back to the sides and bottom board using 2"-long PB screws.

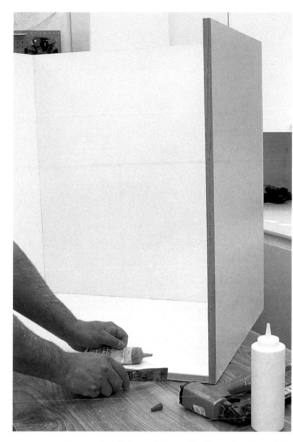

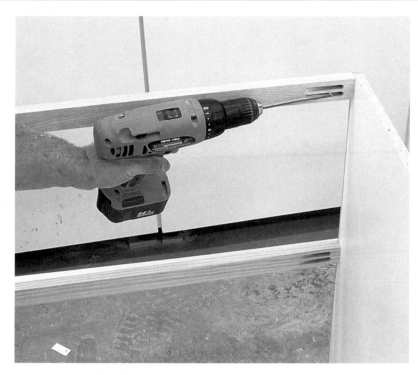

STEP 4 ■ Cut and install the two wood rails F. Secure them to the cabinet with metal angle brackets, screws through the cabinet's side or, as I'm using, pocket screws. The top rail is flush with the top edges of the cabinet sides, and the middle rail is 13½" below the top edges. There should be a 12"-high opening between the two rails for the drawers.

STEP 3 ■ Glue and nail the solid-wood edge strips D and E to the front edges of the side and bottom boards. Fill the nail holes and sand smooth. I'm using oak hardwood for all my edge trim, but any solid wood can be used.

STEP 5 ■ Install the eight right-angle brackets that will be used to secure the cabinet top board. The brackets are attached flush with the top edges of the side, backboard and upper rail. I installed two brackets on each panel and two on the rail.

STEP 6 ■ The four wood wheel pads G can be installed using 1" screws through the bottom board into the pads. They should be installed under the edges of the back and side boards so the load on those panels will shift through the pads and wheels to the floor. Four screws per pad will hold them securely to the cabinet bottom. The locking wheels are attached with 1¼" screws. The wheels I used are 2½" high, and including the pads, the cabinet is 3¼" off the floor.

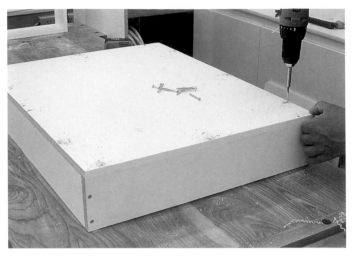

STEP 7 ■ The two drawer boxes are 5" high by 27¾" wide. Cut all drawer parts H, J and K to size. I used ⅝"-thick melamine and secured the butt joints with 2" PB screws. Before assembling the boxes use iron-on edge tape to cover the top edges of the back, front and side boards, as well as the side edges of the bottom board. Attach the sides to the back and front boards using two screws per joint. Keep the screws at least 1" away from the edges of all boards to avoid splitting.

STEP 8 ■ The drawer box bottom board is attached to the bottom edges of the side, back and front boards with 2" PB screws.

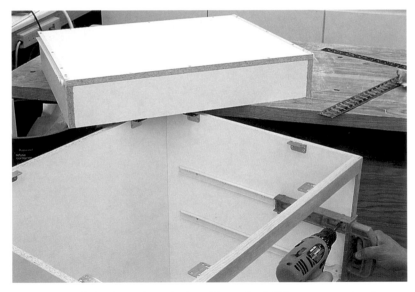

STEP 9 ■ Install the drawer boxes in the cabinet using 22" bottom-mount or, if you prefer, full-extension side-mount glides. The top glides are installed so the bottom of the top drawer box will be 5¾" below the lower edge of the top rail. Use ⅝" screws and follow the installation instructions that come with your hardware.

STEP 10 ■ The drawer faces L are secured to the boxes with four 1" screws. Leave a ¹⁄₁₆" space between the upper and lower drawer face. I used ⅝"-thick melamine PB trimmed with ¼"-thick oak hardwood for my faces. You can use any material to make the drawer faces and doors as long as the finished sizes are the same as the dimensions detailed in the materials list. The drawer faces will overlap the top and middle rail by approximately ½".

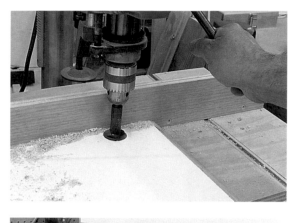

STEP 12 ▪ Drill two 35mm holes in each door, 3" on center from each end. The flat-bottomed hinge holes are drilled ⅛" in from the door's edge.

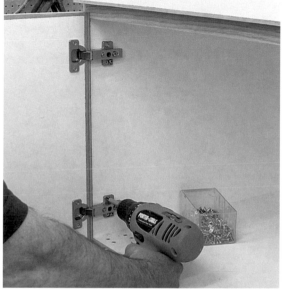

STEP 11 ▪ The door width is calculated by measuring the cabinet's inside width and adding 1". Since I want two doors on my cabinet, I will divide that number by two, (28¾" plus 1" divided by 2), which means I'll need both doors to be 14⅞" wide. The doors are installed flush with the lower edge of the bottom board and overlay the middle rail by about ⅜". I trimmed my door edges with oak, but as mentioned earlier, any material can be used as long as the overall dimensions of the doors are as stated in the materials list.

STEP 13 ▪ Install two standard-opening hinges (between 100° and 120°) in each door and secure them with ½"-long screws, making sure the hinges are 90° to the door's edge. Attach the hinge plates to the hinge body and hold the door against the cabinet in its normally open position with a ⅛" spacer between the door and cabinet edge. Drive screws through the hinge-plate holes to secure the door. Remove the spacer and test the door alignment. Install handles or knobs on the drawers and doors.

STEP 14 ▪ The cabinet top N is a sheet of ⅝"-thick melamine PB with hardwood edge-banding. Attach the edge-banding P and Q with glue and biscuits or screws with wood plugs. Install the top with ⅝" screws through the metal brackets previously installed. There should be a ⅞" overhang on each side, a 1¼" overhang on the front edge and a 2½" overhang at the back edge. The larger overhang on the back will be used to install a wire hole and grommet.

STEP 15 ▪ Drill a wire hole in the back of the top, 1" from the rear edge. Use a wire protector (commonly found at stores that sell electronic supplies). The power cords can pass through the hole and be attached to a power bar.

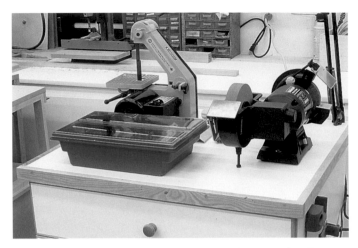

STEP 16 ■ Install your sharpening tools on the cabinet top, keeping them 1" from any edge. I have a 1" belt sander, wet and dry wheel grinder, a water stone bath and a magnifying lamp. I also attached a power bar made by Stanley Tools on the cabinet side. Your equipment will be different from mine, but it should be installed at this time to determine the minimum inside height of the cover.

STEP 17 ■ My cover is the full width and depth of the top, so I need 15" of inside clearance based on my equipment. The side frame will be made with hardwood that's 1" wide by ³/₄" thick. Both ends on frame members R and S are cut at 45° to create a mitered corner at each intersection. The side panels will be ¹/₄"-thick veneer plywood.

Cut a groove that's ¹/₄" wide on one 1" face of each horizontal and vertical ³/₈"-deep frame member. Miter the ends of each member so the long edge is the dimension stated in the materials list. The grooves are on the inside, short dimension of each mitered board. Assemble the two side frames with the panels T installed in the grooves. Use glue and brad nails, then clamp securely until the adhesive cures.

STEP 18 ■ Prepare the four upper cross rails U by ripping a 45° miter along one edge of each board. The face of these rails should be 1¹/₂" wide after ripping the angle. Create a back-and-front upper cross rail assembly by gluing the boards together in pairs at the miter. You should have two assemblies that form a right angle. The boards can be glued and brad nailed or clamped. If you use brads, keep them ³/₈" back from the corner intersection so the edges can be rounded with a router bit.

STEP 19 ■ Join the two sides with the upper cross rails using glue and 2" screws in counterbored holes. These holes can be filled with wood plugs. One 2" screw and glue at each joint will securely hold the rails to the sides.

STEP 20 ■ The two lower cross rails V are also secured with glue and one 2" screw at each end. Counterbore and fill the screw holes with wood plugs.

STEP 21 ■ Use a ¼" roundover bit to ease all the outside edges of the frame members. Do not round over the bottom edges of the cover, because it should sit tight and flat on the cabinet top.

STEP 22 ■ The top panel W and front and back panels X are attached to the inside of the cover with glue and ⅝" brad nails.

STEP 23 ■ Clamp the cover in place on the cabinet so its edges are flush with the outside edges of the top. Use a 28" piano hinge on the back side to secure the cover to the cabinet.

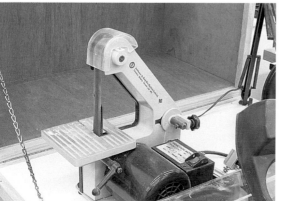

STEP 24 ■ Use a small chain about 12" long to limit the travel of the cover. Then install a handle on the front lower cross rail of the cover so it can be easily raised and lowered.

construction NOTES

You need to deal with two important issues before beginning construction of this sharpening station. First, decide on a comfortable work-surface height and, if it is different from mine, change the height of the sides and backboard to suit your requirements.

Second, the type of equipment that will be mounted on this station will determine the size of the top and clearance requirements for the cover. The belt sander is normally the tallest piece of equipment and is the unit that determines the cover height.

I built my station using ⅝"-thick particleboard and oak hardwood for the trim; however, any sheet material will work just as well. If you do use another sheet material such as MDF or plywood, consider installing a melamine PB or high-pressure laminate top. A smooth surface that's easy to clean is a real bonus.

You may also want to put a self-adhesive foam or rubber gasket on the bottom edge of the cover to further protect the equipment from dust. The cover can be built in another style, with other materials, but a ⅝"-thick melamine PB prototype that I built was very heavy to lift. The frame and panel cover is light and easy to manage, which convinced me that it was the best design for this application.

Finally, change the drawer and door compartments if they don't meet your needs. Three or four small drawers may be more suitable, or for some of you, one drawer will be fine. This project should be designed and built to accommodate your sharpening requirements.

Mobile Workbench and Tool Cabinet

Does your woodworking shop share space with the family car? If you have a garage workshop, this project is perfect for you. The cabinet is mobile, has a large worktable and plenty of tool storage that can be secured with locks.

Many garage woodworkers spend half their time hauling out tools and setting up worktables. A mobile center reduces that lost time because all the tools are in one cabinet. The cabinet is also a worktable, so it can be wheeled to the center of your shop and you're ready to go with tools close at hand.

I used ¾" veneer plywood to build my cabinet, but the project can be built with plywood, MDF or any other ¾" sheet material that's reasonably priced. You'll need about three 4' x 8' sheets of material, locking wheels and drawer glide hardware, so calculate all the costs before you begin.

The storage space on the four pull-outs should hold all of the tools you frequently use. The two large drawers can be used for smaller tools and documents. The mobile feature allows you to roll the cabinet to the side of your shop. Add a few locks as a safety feature, to stop curious youngsters from playing with potentially dangerous equipment.

I built my cabinet so it would do double duty as an outfeed table for a table saw and a handy table at my miter station. In fact, the cabinet can be moved beside any power tool where a table is required. If you want the saw outfeed table feature, verify the height needed before cutting the panels. You should purchase the locking wheel assemblies to determine their height before cutting. The top thickness, side panel height, wheel pads and wheel height will determine the final dimensions of the cabinet.

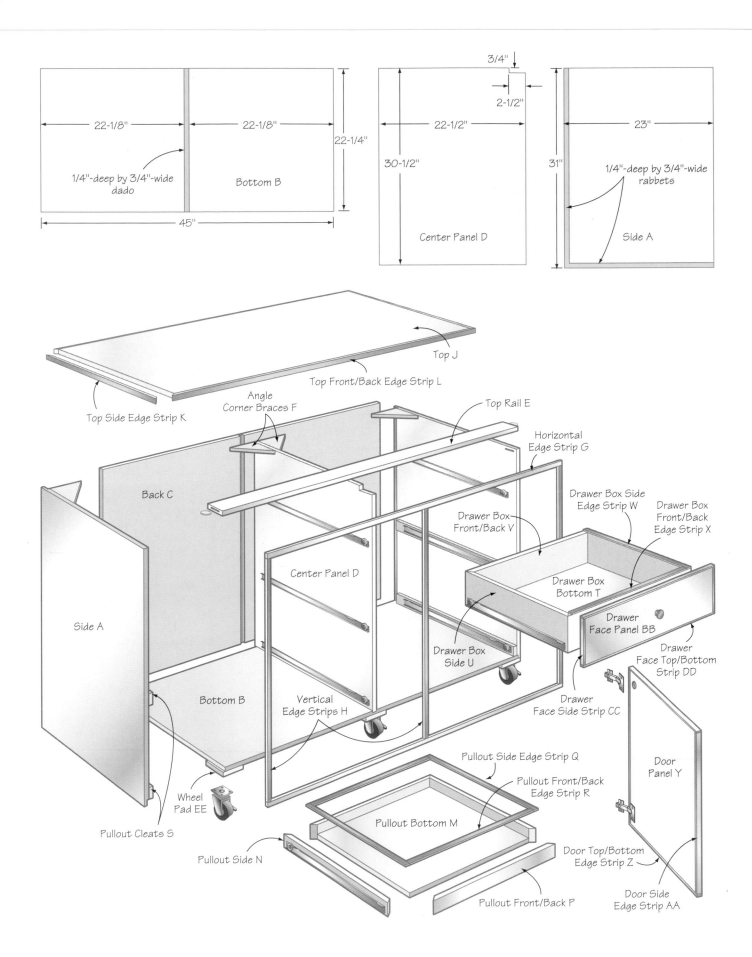

22-1/8" 22-1/8" 22-1/4"

1/4"-deep by 3/4"-wide dado

Bottom B

45"

3/4"

2-1/2"

22-1/2"

30-1/2"

Center Panel D

23"

31"

1/4"-deep by 3/4"-wide rabbets

Side A

Top J

Top Front/Back Edge Strip L

Top Side Edge Strip K

Angle Corner Braces F

Top Rail E

Horizontal Edge Strip G

Back C

Drawer Box Side Edge Strip W

Drawer Box Front/Back Edge Strip X

Drawer Box Front/Back V

Center Panel D

Drawer Box Bottom T

Side A

Drawer Box Side U

Drawer Face Panel BB

Drawer Face Top/Bottom Strip DD

Bottom B

Vertical Edge Strips H

Drawer Face Side Strip CC

Door Panel Y

Wheel Pad EE

Pullout Side Edge Strip Q

Pullout Cleats S

Pullout Front/Back Edge Strip R

Pullout Bottom M

Pullout Side N

Door Top/Bottom Edge Strip Z

Pullout Front/Back P

Door Side Edge Strip AA

materials list ▪ **INCHES**

REFERENCE	QUANTITY	PART	STOCK	THICKNESS	WIDTH	LENGTH	COMMENTS
A	2	sides	plywood	3/4	23	31	
B	1	bottom	plywood	3/4	22 1/4	45	
C	1	back	plywood	3/4	31	45	
D	1	center panel	plywood	3/4	22 1/2	30 1/2	
E	1	top rail	plywood	3/4	2 1/2	44 1/2	
F	4	angle corner braces	hardwood	3/4	3	3	angle-cut
G	2	horizontal edge strips	hardwood	1/4	3/4	46	
H	3	vertical edge strips	hardwood	1/4	3/4	29 1/2	
J	1	top	plywood	3/4	26	48	
K	2	top side edge strips	hardwood	1/4	3/4	26	
L	2	top front/back edge strips	hardwood	1/4	3/4	48 1/2	
M	4	pullout bottoms	plywood	3/4	18 5/8	20 1/2	
N	8	pullout sides	plywood	3/4	2	22	angle-cut
P	8	pullout fronts & backs	plywood	3/4	2	20 1/8	angle-cut
Q	8	pullout side edge strips	hardwood	1/4	3/4	22	
R	8	pullout front/back edge strips	hardwood	1/4	3/4	18 5/8	
S	4	pullout cleats	plywood	3/4	2	22	
T	2	drawer box bottoms	plywood	3/4	19 3/8	20 1/2	
U	4	drawer box sides	plywood	3/4	5	22	angle-cut
V	4	drawer box fronts/backs	plywood	3/4	5	20 7/8	angle-cut
W	4	drawer side edge strips	hardwood	1/4	3/4	22	
X	4	drawer front/back edge strips	hardwood	1/4	3/4	19 3/8	
Y	2	door panels	plywood	3/4	22 1/8	23	
Z	4	door top/bottom edge strips	hardwood	1/4	3/4	22 5/8	
AA	4	door side edge strips	hardwood	1/4	3/4	23	
BB	2	drawer face panels	plywood	3/4	6 3/4	22 1/8	
CC	4	drawer face side strips	hardwood	1/4	3/4	6 3/4	
DD	4	drawer face top/bottom strips	hardwood	1/4	3/4	22 5/8	
EE	6	wheel pads	hardwood	3/4	5	5	

HARDWARE

2" PB screws

Brad nails as detailed

Glue

6 Locking wheels

4 - 22" Drawer glide sets

2 - 22" Full-extension drawer glide sets

4 Knobs

4 - 107° Hidden hinges

24 - 1 1/2"-Long x 5/16"-diameter lag bolts

Finishing nails

#10 Biscuits or dowels

Wood putty

1 1/4" Screws

Iron-on edge tape

5/8" Screws

REFERENCE	QUANTITY	PART	STOCK	THICKNESS	WIDTH	LENGTH	COMMENTS
A	2	sides	plywood	19	584	787	
B	1	bottom	plywood	19	565	1143	
C	1	back	plywood	19	787	1143	
D	1	center panel	plywood	19	572	775	
E	1	top rail	plywood	19	64	1131	
F	4	angle corner braces	hardwood	19	76	76	angle-cut
G	2	horizontal edge strips	hardwood	6	19	1168	
H	3	vertical edge strips	hardwood	6	19	750	
J	1	top	plywood	19	660	1219	
K	2	top side edge strips	hardwood	6	19	660	
L	2	top front/back edge strips	hardwood	6	19	1232	
M	4	pullout bottoms	plywood	19	473	521	
N	8	pullout sides	plywood	19	51	559	angle-cut
P	8	pullout fronts & backs	plywood	19	51	511	angle-cut
Q	8	pullout side edge strips	hardwood	6	19	559	
R	8	pullout front/back edge strips	hardwood	6	19	473	
S	4	pullout cleats	plywood	19	51	559	
T	2	drawer box bottoms	plywood	19	493	521	
U	4	drawer box sides	plywood	19	127	559	angle-cut
V	4	drawer box fronts/backs	plywood	19	127	530	angle-cut
W	4	drawer side edge strips	hardwood	6	19	559	
X	4	drawer front/back edge strips	hardwood	6	19	493	
Y	2	door panels	plywood	19	562	584	
Z	4	door top/bottom edge strips	hardwood	6	19	575	
AA	4	door side edge strips	hardwood	6	19	584	
BB	2	drawer face panels	plywood	19	171	562	
CC	4	drawer face side strips	hardwood	6	19	171	
DD	4	drawer face top/bottom strips	hardwood	6	19	575	
EE	6	wheel pads	hardwood	19	127	127	

HARDWARE

51mm PB screws

Brad nails as detailed

Glue

6 Locking wheels

4 - 559mm Drawer glide sets

2 - 559mm Full-extension drawer glide sets

4 Knobs

4 - 107° Hidden hinges

24 - 38mm-Long x 8mm-diameter lag bolts

Finishing nails

#10 Biscuits or dowels

Wood putty

32mm Screws

Iron-on edge tape

16mm Screws

STEP 1 ▪ Cut the two side panels A to the size shown in the materials list. Form a rabbet that's ¼" deep by ¾" wide on the inside bottom and back edge of each panel.

STEP 2 ▪ Before preparing the bottom B and back C, refer to the construction notes at the end of this chapter regarding cutting the sheets for maximum yield. In the middle of each panel, rout a dado that's ¼" deep by ¾" wide. See the exploded illustration earlier in this chapter for positioning details.

STEP 3 ▪ Attach the sides to the bottom and back panels, being careful to align the center dadoes. Use glue on all the joints and clamp tightly until secure. If you don't have long clamps for the case, use finishing nails to hold the joints until the glue sets.

STEP 4 ▪ The center panel D needs a ¾"-deep by 2½"-long notch at the top front edge to receive the top rail E. Secure the panel with glue and clamps or finishing nails.

STEP 5 ■ The top rail E is secured to the center panel with glue and finishing nails. Carefully align the center panel so there is equal spacing in both sections of the cabinet. I secured both ends of the rail to the side panels using #10 biscuits; however, you can use dowels, pocket holes on the top side or screws and glue.

STEP 6 ■ The rear corners will have right-angle corner braces installed. These will be used to attach the top panel but will also add strength to the mobile case. Attach the four braces F with glue and brad nails.

STEP 8 ■ The top panel J is attached with 1¼" screws through the front rail and four corner braces. Adjust the top so it extends 1¼" past each side and 1½" on the front of the cabinet. Cover the four edges of the top panel with hardwood edge strips K and L using glue and brad nails.

Shop Tip

Don't glue the top in place, so it can be replaced after a few years of use. You might also decide to cover the top panel with a ¼" piece of hardboard that is tacked in place with a few screws. This inexpensive cover can be easily replaced if the top is damaged.

STEP 7 ■ The exposed front edges of the sides, rail and bottom panel are covered with ¼"-thick by ¾"-wide hardwood strips. Use glue and brad nails to attach the strips G and H. Fill the nail holes with wood putty.

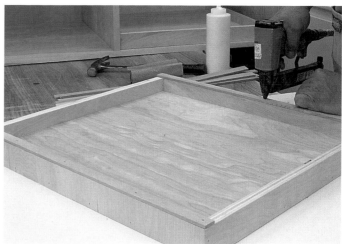

STEP 9 ▪ The four pullouts are constructed using ³⁄₄" plywood veneer or other sheet material. The side, back and front boards are mitered at 45° on each corner. Cut the parts to the sizes detailed in the materials list and assemble each pullout using glue and brad nails. Notice that each pullout is 1³⁄₄" narrower than the cabinet space to allow for drawer glide clearance, and that a ³⁄₄"-thick spacing cleat is needed so the tray will clear the door.

STEP 10 ▪ Trim the top edges of the pullout trays using ¹⁄₄"-thick by ³⁄₄"-wide hardwood strips Q and R. Attach the trim with glue and brad nails, then fill the nail holes with wood putty.

STEP 11 ▪ Both cabinet sections require two spacing cleats S on the door hinge side. This will provide proper clearance for the pullouts. Attach the cleats with 1¹⁄₄" screws. Cover the exposed edges of the plywood with iron-on edge tape or hardwood strips. The cleats are positioned to meet the needs of your storage requirements.

STEP 12 ▪ The four pullout trays are installed using Blum 22" bottom-mount drawer glide hardware. Fit the slides and test for proper operation.

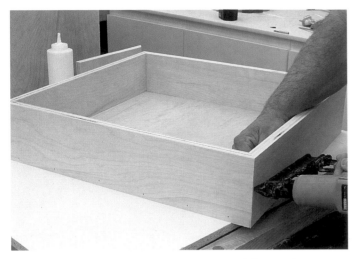

STEP 13 ■ The two drawer boxes are constructed following the same steps as the pullout trays; however, the sides are 5" high and the width is increased by ³/₄" to 20⁷/₈" because they don't have to clear door hinges. The box corners are mitered and assembled using glue and brad nails. The bottom board T is inset like the pullout tray bottoms. Trim the top edges with ¹/₄"-thick hardwood strips W and X, or you can use iron-on edge tape.

STEP 14 ■ I mounted my drawers using Accuride 22" full-extension side-mounted drawer glides. Position the glide hardware so the bottom of each box is 6" below the underside of the top rail.

STEP 15 ■ The finished doors measure 22⁵/₈" wide by 23¹/₂" high after the trim is attached to the panels. Cut the two panels Y and install the trim pieces Z and AA with glue and brad nails. Drill two 35mm holes, ¹/₈" away from the door edge, centered 4" from the top and bottom edge of each door. Install the hinges on the doors with the hinge plates attached. Align each door flush with the bottom edge of the cabinet in its normally open position. Put a ¹/₈"-thick strip of wood between the cabinet front edge and door. Drive ⁵/₈" screws in the plate holes to secure the hinges to the cabinet sides. Remove the ¹/₈" spacing strip and test the operation of each door.

STEP 16 ■ Follow the same assembly steps when building the drawer fronts. The finished size of each front will be 7¹/₄" high by 22⁵/₈" wide. Use 1¹/₄" screws to attach the drawer faces to the boxes. Use a ¹/₈"-thick spacer on top of the door to properly align the drawer faces.

STEP 17 ■ Use glue and two 1¼" screws to install the six wood wheel pads EE on the cabinet base. These pads should be placed at each corner and under the center vertical divider. The load on, and in, the cabinet will be transferred through the cabinet sides and center panel to the wheel pads and onto the wheels to the floor.

STEP 18 ■ Attach one heavy-duty swivel locking wheel on each pad. Use 1½"-long by ⁵⁄₁₆"-diameter lag bolts in pilot holes to secure the wheels.

Cost is a concern when building this cabinet. Making the best use of the sheet materials is important, so plan your cutting diagrams carefully. You should crosscut along the width of the 4' x 8' sheet for large back, bottom and top panels. The top is a full 4', and the other two panels are almost as wide. Use a circular saw to crosscut each panel to a manageable size, then finish the cuts on your table saw.

You can, as I mentioned in the introduction, use any ¾" sheet material. Some reasonably priced plywood can be painted. MDF is inexpensive and a good material to paint, or you may want to use melamine PB. If your shop isn't too damp, any of the mentioned materials would be fine. If the shop is damp and water leaks are possible, you should use plywood.

Align the pullouts in the cabinet to suit your storage requirements. Don't use glue to secure them, so they can be moved should your needs change. The pullout trays work well on the bottom-mount drawer glides, but full-extension hardware can be used. The drawers can also be fitted with regular bottom-mount glides in place of the more expensive full-extension hardware to lessen the cost.

Install the hardwood wheel pads and use six heavy-duty locking wheels that swivel. Four wheels wouldn't support the load properly and may cause the bottom board to sag. The center wheels support a large part of the load and guarantee proper cabinet alignment for the pullouts and drawers.

Saw Outfeed Table and Storage Cabinet

For years my table saw outfeed table was part of a sheet of melamine particleboard (PB) supported by a pair of those inexpensive folding legs you can buy at a home store. The table wasn't very stable and could, and often did, move when I was cutting heavy sheet material on the saw. That safety issue alone made me look toward designing a better outfeed table.

Storage under the metal folding support legs was reduced because of their angle locking system. The legs weren't adjustable, so I was always leveling the table with small pieces of wood. It was a poor outfeed support system and something better, and safer, was needed.

This outfeed table and storage cabinet meets all of my needs. I built it using ³⁄₄"-thick MDF, so it's heavy and stable. It has an adjustable leg system, and the cabinet box provides a great deal of storage space. Adjustable shelves and doors allow me to customize the cabinet for my storage requirements.

The outfeed tabletop I need for my table saw is 3' wide by 6' long. Yours will most likely be different, so change the dimensions to suit your needs. The height will also be different for many of you, so adjust the vertical panel dimension. The cabinet top should be flush with your table saw top.

The cabinet height is a combination of top thickness, vertical panel length and adjustable leg height. If you plan on using an adjustable leg system, buy it before you start and note the height in the middle of the adjustment range. Then cut the side and center panels to the size required based on your table saw height.

The cabinet doesn't require doors if you plan on adding extra shelves to store short lengths of wood. You might want one section with doors for dust-free storage and the other without for small panel storage. There are many ways to configure the cabinet storage section based on your needs. No matter which storage setup you choose, you'll appreciate all the benefits of this solid outfeed table and storage center.

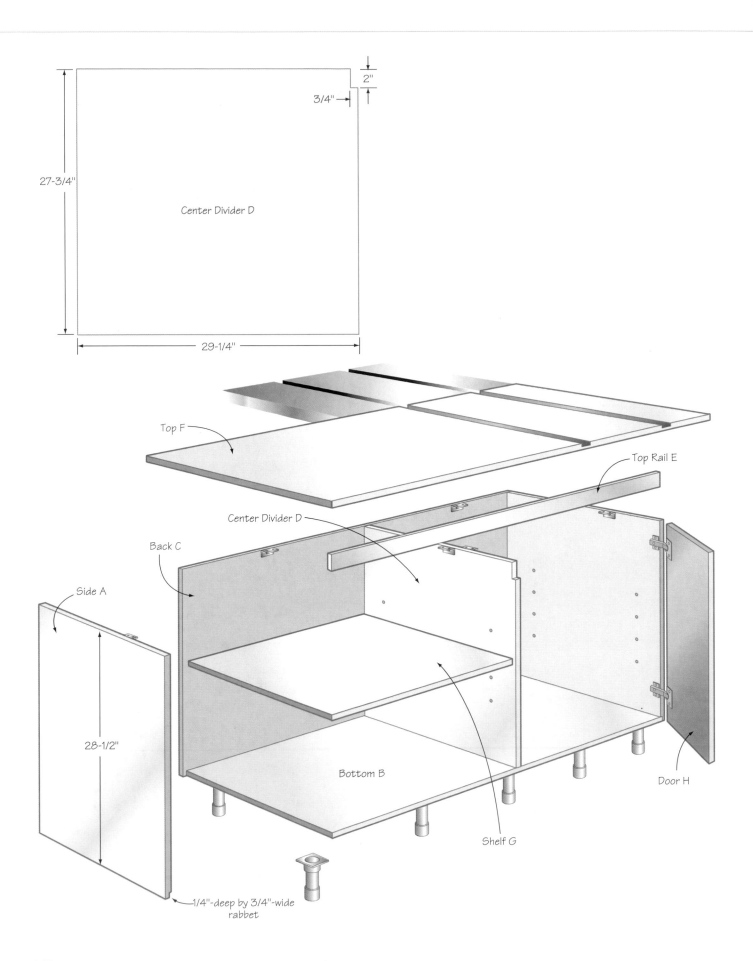

2"

3/4"

27-3/4"

Center Divider D

29-1/4"

Top F

Top Rail E

Center Divider D

Back C

Side A

28-1/2"

Bottom B

Shelf G

Door H

1/4"-deep by 3/4"-wide rabbet

materials list ▪ **INCHES**

REFERENCE	QUANTITY	PART	STOCK	THICKNESS	WIDTH	LENGTH	COMMENTS
A	2	sides	MDF	$3/4$	$29^1/4$	$28^1/2$	
B	1	bottom	MDF	$3/4$	$29^1/4$	$66^1/2$	
C	1	back	MDF	$3/4$	$28^1/2$	$67^1/2$	
D	1	center divider	MDF	$3/4$	$29^1/4$	$27^3/4$	
E	1	top rail	MDF	$3/4$	2	66	
F	1	top	MDF	$3/4$	36	72	
G	2	shelves	MDF	$3/4$	$32^9/16$	29	
H	4	doors	MDF	$3/4$	$16^5/8$	$27^1/2$	

HARDWARE

2" PB screws as detailed

$5/8$" Screws as detailed

Glue

11 Right-angle brackets

10 Adjustable legs

8 Shelf pins

4 – 107° Full-overlay hinges

4 – 107° Half-overlay hinges

8 Standard hinge plates

4 Door handles

$5/8$" Screws

materials list ▪ **MILLIMETERS**

REFERENCE	QUANTITY	PART	STOCK	THICKNESS	WIDTH	LENGTH	COMMENTS
A	2	sides	MDF	19	743	724	
B	1	bottom	MDF	19	743	1689	
C	1	back	MDF	19	724	1715	
D	1	center divider	MDF	19	743	705	
E	1	top rail	MDF	19	51	1676	
F	1	top	MDF	19	914	1829	
G	2	shelves	MDF	19	827	737	
H	4	doors	MDF	19	422	699	

HARDWARE

51mm PB screws as detailed

16mm Screws as detailed

Glue

11 Right-angle brackets

10 Adjustable legs

8 Shelf pins

4 – 107° Full-overlay hinges

4 – 107° Half-overlay hinges

8 Standard hinge plates

4 Door handles

16mm Screws

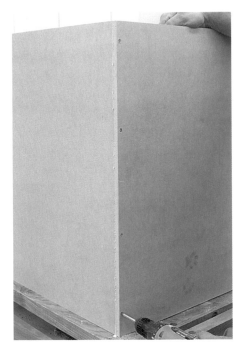

STEP 1 ▪ Cut cabinet sides A to the dimensions listed in the materials list. Drill adjustable shelf-pin holes in the inside face of each side panel. Mark the top of each panel so the first hole distance is referenced from the top edge. This important step will ensure that the center divider's shelf-pin holes will be in alignment with the side panel holes.

STEP 2 ▪ Both side panels require a rabbet that's ¼" deep by ¾" wide on their bottom inside edge. Next, cut the bottom board B to size and join the sides to the bottom board in the rabbets. The joints are secured with glue and four 2" screws on each panel. Remember to drill pilot holes for the screws.

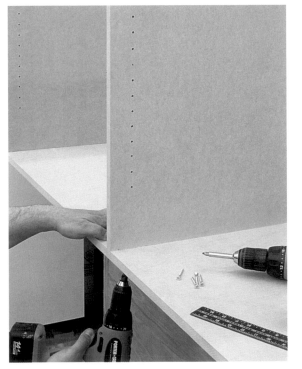

Shop Tip

Keep screws a minimum of 1" away from the end of MDF panels to avoid splitting the material.

STEP 3 ▪ The back C fully overlays or covers the back edges of the sides and bottom board. Use glue and 2" screws, about 6" apart, to secure the back.

STEP 4 ▪ Drill a series of shelf-pin holes on each side of center divider D, being sure to mark and reference the first hole from the top edge of the panel. This will align the side and center divider shelf-pin holes.

Offset the columns of holes on each side of the panel by 1" to avoid drilling through the divider. On the top front edge of the panel, cut a notch that's ¾" deep by 2" high to receive the top rail. Secure the divider in the center of the cabinet, creating two sections that are 32⅝" wide. Use glue and screws through the back and bottom board to secure the divider.

STEP 5 ■ The top rail E is attached to the sides and in the notch of the center panel. The rail is only 2" wide, so screws driven in the end will usually split the MDF. I secured the rail with glue and right-angle brackets using ⅝" screws. Both ends of the rail are aligned with the side's top and face edges. The rail will be secured to the underside of the cabinet top with more right-angle brackets and screws.

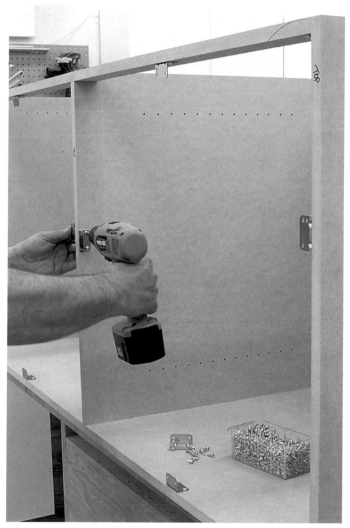

STEP 6 ■ The base support for my table is its adjustable legs. You might opt for a solid base, made with ¾" MDF, but most shop floors are uneven and the adjustable leg is an ideal solution. These legs are available at most woodworking stores.

Attach 10 legs using the manufacturer's fastening recommendations. Two legs are placed under each cabinet side board and two under the center divider. The other four are attached in the middle of each section span.

A base or leg system placed directly under the cabinet's vertical panels will properly transfer the cabinet load to the floor. Set the legs 2" back from the front edge of the cabinet to provide space when someone is standing at the front of the cabinet.

STEP 7 ■ Attach eight right-angle brackets in the center of each panel and on the center of each rail span in every section. These brackets, which will be used to secure the cabinet top, should be flush with the top edge of each panel.

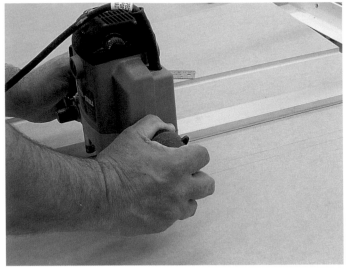

STEP 8 ■ The top board F is ¾"-thick MDF. Secure it to the cabinet using screws through the previously installed brackets.

The sides overhang the cabinet by 2¼". The front overhang is 1", and the top extends past the back of the cabinet by 5". I've offset the front and back overhang so the cabinet won't interfere with my vacuum system behind the table saw. Adjust the top overhang to suit your shop setup.

STEP 9 ■ Place the cabinet in its permanent location and level the top to the table saw top. Use a router and straightedge to cut two dadoes in the cabinet top that are in line with the miter slide tracks of the saw. Adjust the dado depth to match the track depth on the saw.

STEP 10 ■ I installed two shelf boards G in my cabinet, but your storage needs may be different, so install as many as needed. The best shelf pin for this application has a full-metal shaft to support heavy loads. Install the pins in the drilled holes and test fit the shelves.

STEP 11 ▪ The cabinet can be left as an open shelving unit or have doors installed. The doors are attached using 100° to 120° hidden hinges. Cut the four doors H, then drill two 35mm-diameter holes in each that are 4" on center from each end and ⅛" away from the door edge. Hinge holes are approximately ½" deep, but test fit the hinges to ensure they are seated correctly.

STEP 12 ▪ The hinges on the two outside doors are full-overlay models, and the four on the inside doors are half-overlay. Install the hinges, with hinge plates attached, then mount the doors on the cabinets.

Hold the door in its normally open position, flush with the bottom edge of the base board. Place a ⅛"-thick strip of wood between the door edge and cabinet front edge. This spacing is needed to properly set the door-to-cabinet gap. Drive screws through the hinge-plate holes into the cabinet to secure the doors. Adjust the doors if necessary so there's a 1/16" gap in the center of each pair. Finally, install four handles of your choice.

You can avoid using a combination of half- and full-overlay hinges by installing two center dividers. Follow the same installation steps for the second divider, being sure to leave equal spacing in both sections of the cabinet. You won't have to worry about offsetting shelf-pin hole columns with two dividers, and standard full-overlay hinges can be used on all the doors. Door width will change with the two-divider system, however. Measure the inside width of the cabinet, add 1" to that dimension and divide by 2; that's the required width of each door.

The cabinet interior is easily modified to suit your needs. Vertical dividers can be installed to create more than two sections, extra shelves can be added and doors can be installed on all or one section only. The cabinet can be easily customized for your shop.

If you plan on storing a lot of heavy items on the shelves, I suggest you use ¾"-thick plywood in place of the MDF. This two-section cabinet design requires wide shelves that can bend with heavy loads. If the shelves will be used to support heavy material or equipment, consider building the cabinet with three sections as a possible option.

As previously discussed, this cabinet design suits my table saw. Most saws are close in style and dimension, but you will have to make minor dimensional changes to suit your equipment. You might also consider mounting this cabinet on locking wheels if your table saw is mobile; however, you will need a level workshop floor for this option.

Shop-Made 12″ Disc Sander

This project is inexpensive and easy to build, providing you have an electric motor lying around your shop, or you plan on picking one up at the next neighborhood garage sale.

The cabinet, motor support and adjustable table system are built using ¾″ MDF sheet material. A few pieces of hardware such as screws, hinges and a motor pulley are all that is needed to build this handy 12″ disc sander.

I will be using the sander to round over small parts, sand flat edges and smooth band saw cuts. My wife wants this sander for her craftwork because it's a great tool for finish-sanding dozens of small parts. The disc runs quietly and quickly removes material with the proper paper grit.

The self-adhesive 12″-diameter sanding discs are available at woodworking stores. I use an 80-grit paper for general work and 150-grit paper for finer work. This disc sander is a safe tool, so woodworkers of all ages can use it. The platform is close to the disc and is an ideal support for your work, but it also serves as a safety guard should the disc loosen.

The woodworkers who have dropped into my shop while I was building this sander were impressed with the project, and a few more are being built. All my friends are hunting through old motors that they've been storing for years. Finally, a use for that electric motor you knew couldn't be thrown out!

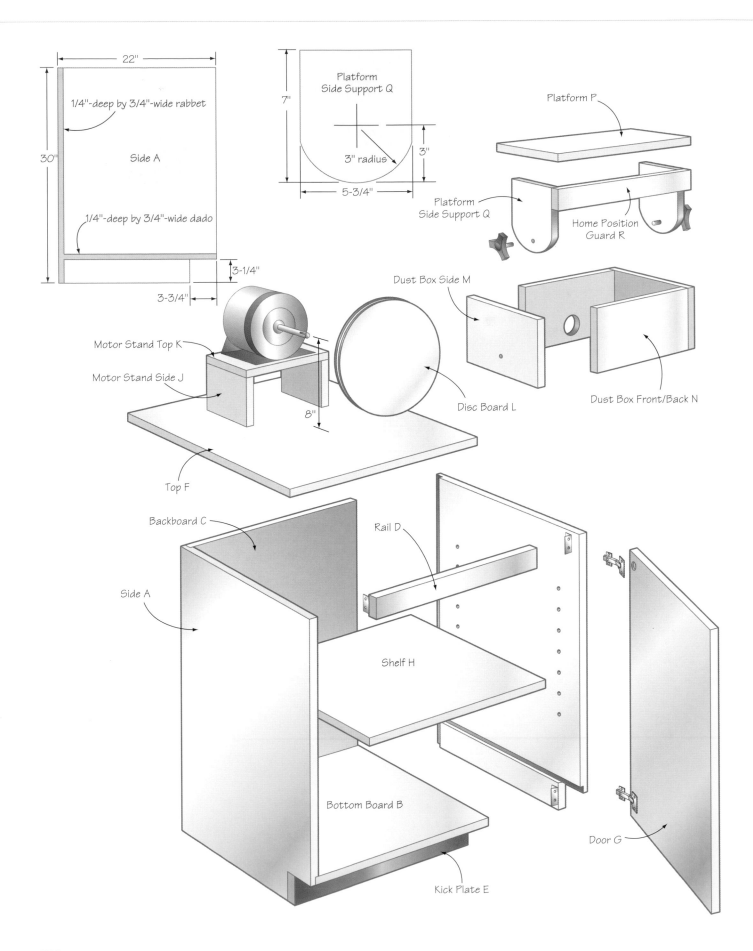

22"

1/4"-deep by 3/4"-wide rabbet

Side A

30"

1/4"-deep by 3/4"-wide dado

3-1/4"

3-3/4"

Platform
Side Support Q

7"

3" radius

3"

5-3/4"

Platform P

Platform
Side Support Q

Home Position
Guard R

Dust Box Side M

Motor Stand Top K

Motor Stand Side J

8"

Disc Board L

Dust Box Front/Back N

Top F

Backboard C

Rail D

Side A

Shelf H

Bottom Board B

Door G

Kick Plate E

materials list ▪ **INCHES**

REFERENCE	QUANTITY	PART	STOCK	THICKNESS	WIDTH	LENGTH	COMMENTS
A	2	sides	MDF	3/4	22	30	
B	1	bottom board	MDF	3/4	16	22	
C	1	backboard	MDF	3/4	16	26	
D	1	rail	MDF	3/4	2	15 1/2	
E	1	kick plate	MDF	3/4	3 1/4	17	
F	1	top	MDF	3/4	19	23 1/2	
G	1	door	MDF	3/4	16 1/2	26	
H	2	shelves	MDF	3/4	15 7/16	21	
J	2	motor stand sides	MDF	3/4	4 1/4	7	
K	1	motor stand top	MDF	3/4	10	7	
L	1	disc board	plywood	3/4	12 1/2	12 1/2	
M	2	dust box sides	MDF	3/4	8	6	
N	2	dust box front & back	MDF	3/4	13	6	
P	1	platform	MDF	3/4	8	18	
Q	2	platform side supports	MDF	3/4	5 3/4	7	
R	1	home position guard	MDF	3/4	3	16 1/16	

HARDWARE

1 1/2" Screws as detailed

Glue

8 Right-angle brackets

8 Shelf pins

2 – 107° Full-overlay hinges

1 Motor

1 Motor pulley

2 Knobs with 1/4" x 20" threaded shafts

2 T-nuts 1/4" x 20"

1 Door handle or knob

5/8" Screws

1 1/2" Screws

materials list ▪ **MILLIMETERS**

REFERENCE	QUANTITY	PART	STOCK	THICKNESS	WIDTH	LENGTH	COMMENTS
A	2	sides	MDF	19	559	762	
B	1	bottom board	MDF	19	406	559	
C	1	backboard	MDF	19	406	660	
D	1	rail	MDF	19	51	394	
E	1	kick plate	MDF	19	82	432	
F	1	top	MDF	19	483	597	
G	1	door	MDF	19	419	660	
H	2	shelves	MDF	19	392	533	
J	2	motor stand sides	MDF	19	108	178	
K	1	motor stand top	MDF	19	254	178	
L	1	disc board	plywood	19	318	318	
M	2	dust box sides	MDF	19	203	152	
N	2	dust box front & back	MDF	19	330	152	
P	1	platform	MDF	19	203	457	
Q	2	platform side supports	MDF	19	146	178	
R	1	home position guard	MDF	19	76	408	

HARDWARE

38mm Screws as detailed

Glue

8 Right-angle brackets

8 Shelf pins

2 – 107° Full-overlay hinges

1 Motor

1 Motor pulley

2 Knobs with 1/4" x 20" threaded shafts

2 T-nuts 6mm x 508mm

1 Door handle or knob

16mm Screws

38mm Screws

STEP 1 ■ Cut the sides A to size and drill two columns of holes for adjustable shelves on the inside face of each panel. Start the columns 4" from the top and end them about 4" from the bottom edges. Each column should be 2" in from the panel edge.

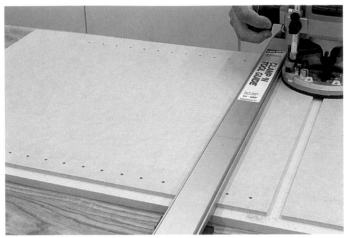

STEP 2 ■ Rout a ¼"-deep by ¾"-wide rabbet on the back inside face of each side panel A. They also need a ¼"-deep by ¾"-wide dado to accept the bottom board. The top edge of each dado should be 4" above the bottom edge of the side panel.

STEP 3 ■ The side panels also require a 3¼"-high by 3¾"-deep notch on their bottom front edge for the kick plate. Use a jigsaw, scroll saw or band saw to cut the notches.

STEP 4 ■ The bottom board B is attached to the side panels in the previously cut dadoes. Apply glue to the dadoes and clamp the sides to the bottom board until the adhesive sets.

STEP 6 ■ The upper rail D can be attached with small biscuits, dowels or brackets and glue as I'm using. The top edge of the rail is flush with the top edges of the side panels.

STEP 5 ■ The backboard C is installed in the two rabbets with glue. The assembly is clamped and 1½" screws are driven through the bottom board into the lower edge of the backboard. Once again, wait until the glue sets before removing the clamps.

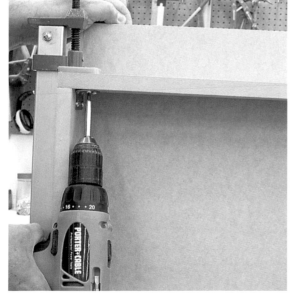

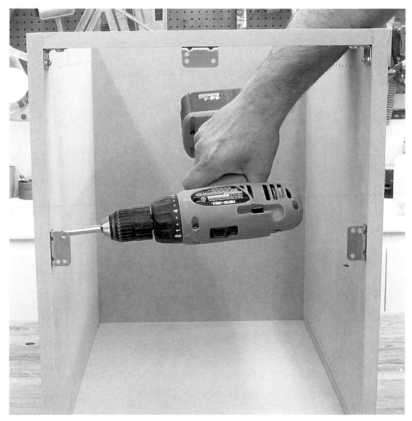

STEP 7 ■ The kick plate E can also be secured with glue and right-angle brackets on the back side.

STEP 8 ■ Install four right-angle brackets using ⅝" screws. The top of these brackets should be flush with the top edges of the sides, back and front rail. The brackets will be used to secure the cabinet top board.

STEP 10 ▪ Install the hinges, with their hinge plates attached, on the door. Hold the door G in its normally open position, flush with the bottom edge of the base board B. Place a ⅛"-thick strip of wood between the door edge and cabinet front edge. This spacing is needed to properly set the door-to-cabinet gap. Drive screws through the hinge-plate holes into the cabinet to secure the door. Install a knob or handle of your choice, then cut and install the two shelf boards H.

STEP 9 ▪ Place the top board F on the cabinet with a 1" overhang on each side and a 1½" overhang on the front edge. The back edge is flush with the outside face of the backboard. Use ⅝" screws in the previously installed brackets to secure the top.

STEP 11 ▪ Build a stand, as shown, to raise the center of the motor shaft 8" above the cabinet top. Leave about 10" in front of the stand. Your motor will probably be different from mine, so exact measurements are not given. The suggested dimensions should suit most electric motor sizes. See the construction notes at the end of this chapter for information on selecting a motor.

Use glue and 1½" screws through the underside of the top board to secure the motor stand. Attach the motor to the stand using whichever method is best suited to the motor you are using. My motor came equipped with a bracket, so I bolted the assembly through the stand top K.

STEP 12 ▪ For the disc board L, draw a 12⅛"-diameter circle on a ¾"-thick piece of plywood with a compass. Cut the circle as accurately as possible using a band saw, jigsaw or scroll saw. Measure the diameter of your pulley and draw a circle matching that size on the wood disc using the same center point.

Drill four holes through the pulley and attach it to the back face of the wood disc. Use screws that are long enough to anchor all the way into the thickness of the wood disc without puncturing the front face.

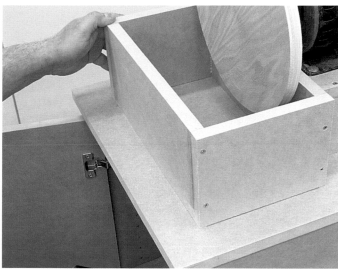

STEP 13 ■ Install the disc and pulley assembly on the motor shaft, then lock it securely using the fastening system on your pulley. Wire the motor to a switch box and attach the box on the motor stand with screws.

Start the motor and true the disc using sandpaper. The disc should be sanded to 12" in diameter. Install 12"-diameter self-adhesive sandpaper to the front face of the wood disc.

STEP 14 ■ Build a simple dust box with $3/4$"-thick MDF that's $14\frac{1}{2}$"-wide by 8"-deep. The box should be 6" high and is assembled using glue and $1\frac{1}{2}$" screws. Align the box on the cabinet top board with equal spacing on both sides. You will have to temporarily remove the disc to install the dust box. Secure the box to the cabinet with $1\frac{1}{2}$" screws through the underside of the top.

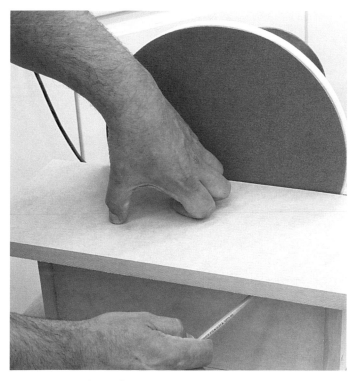

STEP 15 ■ Cut the platform P and place it on the dust box with equal spacing on each side and $1/8$" away from the sanding disc face. Trace the outline of the dust box on the underside of the platform.

STEP 16 ■ Cut platform side supports Q, and draw a 3"-radius arc on the bottom edge of each board. Use a belt sander to form the arc on each support by sanding to the compass lines. Use glue and three $1\frac{1}{2}$" screws to attach the side supports to the platform Q, keeping $1/32$" away from the lines.

The home position guard R is secured to the sides of the platform supports with glue and screws. This guard will keep most of the dust in the box and help align the platform at its home position.

The electric motor should be rated at ⅓ horsepower or more. These are common motors and should be available for a reasonable price at garage sales and flea markets.

The ⅓-horsepower motor I installed is powerful enough to handle my sanding requirements. However, you might be fortunate enough to find a good ½- or ¾-horsepower motor that will have the power to tackle any sanding job.

If you're not comfortable wiring the motor and switch unit, have someone who is familiar with electrical work complete this part of the project. Also, many motors have a reversible rotation feature so you might want to change the direction. My motor rotates counterclockwise as you face the disc, but it doesn't seem to matter which direction it rotates because the sander performs equally well in either rotation.

The cabinet can be built with any sheet material. I have one door and adjustable shelves for sandpaper storage, but drawers can be installed just as easily. The vacuum feature works well and does reduce the dust level that can be a serious concern with this tool. I think it's a worthwhile feature and suggest you have the vacuum on when using the sander.

STEP 17 ■ Block the platform assembly so the top surface is aligned with the center of the sanding disc. Use a T-nut and knob with a threaded shaft on each side support to lock the platform in place. The home position guard will reference the platform at 90° to the sanding disc face, and the curved bottoms on the side supports will allow you to move the platform to any angle. The assembly can also be quickly tipped back to permit easy sandpaper removal and installation.

STEP 18 ■ Tip the platform assembly back and remove the sanding disc. Drill a 2¼"-diameter hole in the backboard of the dust box. You can easily access the backboard through the rear of the motor stand. A standard 2¼"-diameter vacuum hose can now be attached to the dust box.

suppliers

Many suppliers have contributed products, material and technical support during the project-building phase of this book. I appreciate how helpful they've been and recommend these companies without hesitation.

ADAMS & KENNEDY – THE WOOD SOURCE
6178 Mitch Owen Road
P.O. Box 700
Manotick, Ontario K4M 1A6
613-822-6800
www.wood-source.com
Wood supply

DELTA MACHINERY
90 Passmore Lane
Jackson, Tennessee 38305
800-223-7278 (in US)
800-463-3582 (in Canada)
www.deltawoodworking.com
Woodworking tools

EXAKTOR WOODWORKING TOOLS, INC.
4 Glenbourne Park
Markham, Ontario L6C1G9
800-387-9789
www.excal-tools.com
Accessories for the table saw

HOUSE OF TOOLS LTD.
100 Mayfield Common Northwest
Edmonton, Alberta T5P 4B3
780-944-9600
www.houseoftools.com
Woodworking tools and hardware

JESSEM TOOL COMPANY
171 Robert T. E. # 7 & # 8
Penetanguishene, Ontario L9M 1G9
800-436-6799
www.jessem.com
Rout-R-Slide and Rout-R-Lift

LEE VALLEY TOOLS LTD.

USA:
P.O. Box 1780
Ogdensberg, New York 13669-6780
800-267-8735

Canada:
P.O. Box 6295, Station J
Ottawa, Ontario K2A 1T4
800-267-8761
www.leevalley.com
Fine woodworking tools and hardware

PORTER CABLE
4825 Highway 45 North
P.O. Box 2468
Jackson, Tennessee 38302-2468
800-487-8665
www.porter-cable.com
Woodworking tools

RICHELIEU HARDWARE
7900 West Henri-Bourassa
Ville St. Laurent, Quebec H4S 1V4
800-619-5446 (in US)
800-361-6000 (in Canada)
www.richelieu.com
Hardware supplies

ROCKLER WOODWORKING AND HARDWARE
4365 Willow Drive
Medina, Minnesota 55340
800-279-4441
www.rockler.com
Woodworking tools and hardware

TENRYU AMERICA, INC.
7964 Kentucky Drive, Suite 12
Florence, Kentucky 41042
800-951-7297
www.tenryu.com
Saw blades

TOOL TREND LTD.
140 Snow Boulevard
Concord, Ontario L4K 4L1
416-663-8665
Woodworking tools and hardware

VAUGHAN & BUSHNELL MANUFACTURING
11414 Maple Avenue
Hebron, Illinois 60034
815-648-2446
www.vaughanmfg.com
Hammers and other tools

WOLFCRAFT NORTH AMERICA
1222 W. Ardmore Avenue
P.O. Box 687
Itasca, Illinois 60143
630-773-4777
www.wolfcraft.com
Woodworking hardware and accessories

WOODCRAFT
P.O. Box 1686
Parkersburg, West Virginia 26102-1686
800-225-1153
www.woodcraft.com
Woodworking hardware and accessories

index

B

Base- and Wall-Mounted Cabinets,
8-17
  materials lists, 11

C

Cabinet sizes, 13
Cabinets, Base- and Wall-Mounted, 8-17
  materials lists, 11
Crosscutting sled, 66-67
  materials lists, 66

D

Disc Sander, Shop-Made 12", 118-
126
Door sizes, 12, 53
Drawers, 16-17
Drill press accessories, 89
Drill Press Center, 80-89
  materials lists, 83
Dust collection, 79

F

Fence platforms, building, 36
Finishing, 27
Frameless cabinetry, 14

H

Hardwood, 27
Height, cabinet, 54, 65, 79, 99

M

Materials lists
  Base- and Wall-Mounted Cabi-
  nets, 11
  Drill Press Center, 83
  Mobile Table Saw Center, 57-58
  Mobile Workbench and Tool
  Cabinet, 103-104
  Multifunction Power Tool Cabi-
  net, 43
  Power Miter Saw Station, 31-32
  Power Tool Storage Station, 51
  Practical Workbench, 21
  Router Table Cabinet, 71-72
  Saw Outfeed Table and Storage
  Cabinet, 113

Shop-Made 12" Disc Sander,
  118-126
Tool Sharpening and Maintenance Station, 93-94
Mobile Table Saw Center, 54-65
  materials lists, 57-58
Mobile Workbench and Tool Cabinet, 100-109
  materials lists, 103-104
Multifunction Power Tool Cabinet,
  40-47
  materials lists, 43

P

Panels, splitting, 33, 114
Pilot holes, 33
Power Miter Saw Station, 28-39
  materials lists, 31-32
Power Tool Cabinet, Multifunction,
  40-47
Power Tool Storage Station, 48-53
  materials lists, 51
Practical Workbench, 18-27
  Materials lists, 21
Projects
  Base- and Wall-Mounted Cabi-
  nets, 8-17
  crosscutting sled, 66-67
  Drill Press Center, 80-89
  Mobile Table Saw Center, 54-65
  Mobile Workbench and Tool
  Cabinet, 100-109
  Multifunction Power Tool Cabi-
  net, 40-47
  Power Miter Saw Station, 28-39
  Power Tool Storage Station, 48-
  53
  Practical Workbench, 18-27
  Router Table Cabinet, 68-79
  Saw Outfeed Table and Storage
  Cabinet, 110-117
  Shop-Made 12" Disc Sander,
  118-126
  Tool Sharpening and Mainte-
  nance Station, 90-99

R

Router Table Cabinet, 68-79
  materials lists, 71-72

S

Sanding drum, 89
Saw Outfeed Table and Storage
  Cabinet, 110-117
  materials lists, 113
Shop-Made 12" Disc Sander, 118-
126
  materials lists, 118-126
Suppliers, 127

T

Tool Sharpening and Maintenance
  Station, 90-99
  materials lists, 93-94

W

Wheels, support, 109